Manners
Maketh
Man

Adventures of a Bo School Boy

Manners Maketh Man:
Adventures of a Boy School Boy
Copyright © 2012 by Siaka Kroma

ISBN: 978-9988-1-4754-9

Printed in Ghana

Sierra Leonean Writers Series
c/o Mallam O. & J. Enterprises
120 Kissy Road, Freetown, Sierra Leone
publisher@sl-writers-series.org /
writersseries.sl@gmail.com

i

Author's Note

This book has been adapted from *A Corner of Time* written by the author for a different audience. Sections that may be identical have been rewritten to enrich the theme and focus of this story. In most cases, names have been changed to enhance anonymity. Also, new episodes and fictitious characters have been added.

Acknowledgement

I am thankful to my editor Esther Nyaga and two meticulous reviewers: Prof. Sheik Umar Kamarah and my friend, Dr. Sorie Conteh. Whatever flaws remain in the book can only be attributed to me.

Dedication
This one is for my boys:
Kaps, Kanjiko, Ken, and Thomas.

Chapter 1

HELLO

My name is Bandami; BandamiSenessie. Bandami in Mende is a question, asking, 'Where do you lay him?' So mine is the only name I know that is a question and should end with a question mark, but it does not. I am an old Bo School Boy. My admission number, 1XX3. The number of digits indicates my generation; the Xs represent other identifying numbers in that generation. My story begins in a small village in the Kailahun District, in the eastern part of Sierra Leone.

I was born on the day the fearsome *Nyangomba* attacked the sun, an epic cosmic battle, a solar eclipse, that lasted a full hour. While it raged, all the villagers came out to support the sun, beating on pots, pans, drums, anything that could produce a raucous distraction for *Nyangomba*. At last *Nyangomba* relented; the sun triumphed, and the people regained their sunlight. It was the main topic of conversation for the rest of the day; it eclipsed the news that MattuYeppeh, my mother, had given birth to a boy. In the coming days, however, the latter event would overshadow all other news as villagers in Malema traded the details of my birth. I came as a heavy child, too big for my young mother. People who called to pay their respect would ask my parents, 'Bandami?' meaning 'Where do you lay him?' With time this became my name, BandamiSenessie, effectively suppressing my true name Sondifu, given four days after my birth, as was the custom.

During the Second World War, food was scarce among the local people. People had to contribute a quota of rice to support the troops overseas. This was known as *kotabei* (quota rice). After giving the *kotabei*, many families had little to feed themselves. My parents were among those whose resources were so stretched. This situation was however eased by a kind stranger. A contingent of the First Battalion, Royal Sierra Leone Military Forces had camped two miles out of Malema, a small town in the Yawei chiefdom in Sierra Leone. The town was situated on a newly constructed road that connected the diamond fields of the Kono District, twenty one miles north, to the railway station thirty miles south of Malema. The army had camped there to protect the mines from a potential attack. During one of his excursions into the town, an army officer chanced upon my mother dutifully carrying a load on her head. The officer was struck by two things: one, the fact that the load on my mother's head was a baby and two, when he saw how nourished this baby appeared when most people in the community were lacking in the staple food. Thereupon, he ordered a regular supply of army rations for my mother. My mother and I enjoyed this kind gesture until the war ended and the battalion moved out.

I was sent to live with my grandparents the moment I could take my first steps. Medicine men in Malema had warned my parents that my life was in danger from witchcraft. The witches and wizards in the village were planning to 'eat' me. My parents, believing what they had been told, and not bearing the thought of losing me, decided in the middle of the night to take me to Mano, three miles away, where my mother's family lived. There I stayed with my grandfather and my grandmother; I should say my grandmothers because that was what all of my grandfather's wives were to me.

My grandfather was JemisiGomna, his real name, NgevauLahai. JemisiGomna was a nickname given to him by his peers when Governor Sir James Shaw Hayes toured the Kailahun district and passed through Mano. My grandfather was in his teens then. The nickname started as a tease; then it stuck for the rest of my grandfather's life. Even when he became chief after his father, he remained Gomna to most people. Only his mother and elders in the town called him Ngevau out of respect for his own grandfather who had borne that name before him.

Colonial Sierra Leone had a protectorate and a colony, each differently administered. The protectorate was demarcated into provinces, districts, and chiefdoms, with a descending order of powers and authority. Provincial and district administrators were *Puubla* (British). The chiefdoms were ruled by traditional rulers known as paramount chiefs. Each chiefdom was further subdivided into sections headed by section chiefs and then the village or town chief. These chiefs were the traditional rulers in the scheme scholars' dubbed 'indirect rule.'

Colonization created new challenges and opportunities, as well as new strategies for survival. Those who understood the new game fared well while those who did not or who resisted change perished or stagnated. My grandfather was one of the first chiefs who understood this new game, the requirement to educate children the white man's way. He sent two sons to school one of whom went on to join the army. At the time of my birth, Uncle Jusu was away in Burma fighting in World War II. His second son, Uncle Kava, was in a boarding school run by the Evangelical United Brethren Church (EUB) twenty-four miles to the north. My uncles being sent to school marked the turning point in the history of our family.

Life with my grandfather was both entertaining and educative. I went everywhere with him. I got glimpses into how the Mende educated their children, settled disputes, and how male adults spent their evenings. Storytelling was a regular form of entertainment. Adults took turns sharing their stories in the presence of children. These intergenerational interactions through which the myths, legends, and true stories of the people were disseminated were the means by which the young were educated by the elders. History was transmitted this way.

Adults also played postprandial games that both entertained and engaged children. One game that I remember with fondness featured the *koningei*, a string instrument that was like a bow, only that the string on the bow was what produced the sound. The player used a flexible straw to strike the string at various points while holding it against his open mouth. Variations in the sound so produced depended on the narrowing and widening of the player's mouth. The instrument was often used to accompany games. In one game, one or two people would be made to leave the group; a riddle would be told in their absence. They would have to guess at the riddle on their return. The *koningei* served to help them know when they were hot or cold on their clues. Things were also hidden and found in a similar fashion.

Cases were also frequently adjudicated after the evening meal in the presence of children. One case that remains in my memory involved the issue of ownership. FayiaFangamandu, a Kissi man, had settled in Mano and married Bondu, a daughter of KombaNdomahina, a Kono man who had also settled in Mano. They had all become an integral part of the Mano community. One evening, Bondu brought a suit to my grandfather claiming that her husband had seized a kerosene tin of palm oil from her and sold it without her consent and knowledge. As usual, Bondu was advised to return after the evening dinner. She did and the matter was formally put before my grandfather and his assessors. Fayia was summoned and asked to respond to the complaint. In response, he admitted selling Bondu's palm oil but in his defense asserted that Bondu was his wife and therefore he did not need her permission to sell her oil; that the oil equally belonged to him for the same reason.

After his defense, my grandfather decided to settle the matter without bothering the other elders. He said to them, "*Ye ji ta mu tewekutu ma* (We will cut this one short)." He then addressed Fayia.

"Fayia, our people say, 'You may own the hen but the hen owns her egg, for only she can decide whether to hatch it or not.' You the owner have nothing to do about that. Similarly Fayia, Bondu may be your wife but what she owns is her own; she is not a slave, mind you." Then he asked the elders, "Is it not so, family members?" They all nodded their heads in the affirmative. And so the case was decided in Bondu's favor. Fayia was ordered to pay restitution to his wife. In disgust some muttered, "What kind of a man would snatch food from a baby?"

Uncle Jusu came from the war in 1945. My first memory of him was that of a tall man dressed in the most horrifying clothes. He walked with something on his feet which nobody in the village wore. Everybody walked barefoot. His appearance put me in awe of him. I instinctively took cover with Uncle Kava, who I knew very well because he always came home for his holidays. In any case he never dressed in the ridiculous way that Uncle Jusu dressed. Nothing Uncle Jusu did could entice me to go near him.

From the start, Uncle Jusu was very fond of me and he devised ingenuous ways to get my attention. Eventually what worked was to carry me while I was sleeping. I would wake up in his arms and see his smiling face looking down at me. With time, a friendship of sorts developed between us, a friendship that grew stronger as he led me into the secrets of his world. He would invite me to eat with him. He would send me to fetch his boots, his watch, or his cigarettes. The other children of the household envied me, and the more they did, the more I grew to like what I was being made to do. After spending six months in the village, Uncle Jusu disappeared again just when I had grown to really like him. He no longer lived in the village with us instead he came occasionally. Our interactions would resume when he came and cease when he left. Even so, he always had something for me when he visited.

Another grandmother I was attached to was Mama Satta, my father's mother. From time to time she would come and release me from my exile home and take me back only for my parents to come and pick me up later. She never relented. She came regularly. While I lived with her, she did all she could to make my life eventful. She had converted to Christianity and did not believe in witchcraft the way my father and mother did. She would therefore defy their wishes and take me to Malema only for my parents to take me back at the earliest opportunity. She attended church services and classes regularly and she would take me along with her. On Wednesday nights we would go to the small village church for one of the class meetings. At the end they would call out names and people would answer and announce how much they had for class that evening. They would call my grandmother, "SattaSenessie" and she would answer, "*Plejen pay torpenji* (Present, paying three pence)." After service, the members would process in song around the village past our *peewa* (big house) where my grandmother lived with the wives of her nephews and cousins. The group would bid her goodnight and disperse to their own homes. Mama Satta was like the grand matron for most in the village.

I played happily between the forces of witchcraft and the attractions of the village church. The latter were mainly the songs and the stories both of which were invariably rendered with an African tint. Numerous didactic songs had been composed in Mende to challenge the local beliefs, songs like '*NgiBaomoiloa'* (I have seen the Saviour) with the refrain "*Ngetortorgbeboma, ngiBaomoiloa* (I don't consult diviners anymore, I have seen the Saviour)." I enjoyed dancing to the rhythm of such songs as we processed back home.

On other evenings, I was attracted to displays in the town square, displays like the dress rehearsals of *Bondo* initiates, the roving storyteller, or the odd magician. Unlike church events, all of these occurred in the season of plenty, after the harvest. Mama Satta did not mind my attending them. What she detested was *Kemei*, the witch hunter. Whenever one was in town it always proved a struggle between Grandma and me. I would sneak to the dance and as many times as I did, she would fetch me back till, overcome by tiredness, I would go to sleep on her laps.

In my last year with Mama Satta, a magician came to town whose feats left people talking long after he had gone. He came to Malema shortly after Christmas and stayed a good two months at the largesse of a mystified and captivated audience. In his first week he played the usual tricks: handkerchiefs, rings, and rabbits. In that same week, he claimed that he could kill someone and keep that dead person in communication with living people, then bring him or her back to life. The whole town dared him do that. On the Friday of that week, the magician 'shot' a young man in front of the curious audience. To everyone's horror the man fell down dead. He was then carried away by a group of young men to his *gborji* (shrine), a spot by the main road he had established as his sacred grounds forbidden to all but a few young men. For days following the 'shooting' anyone who passed along the main road would be greeted by name by *Ndoumoi*, (the man beneath the earth). *Ndoumoi* could even tell remarkable details like the type and colour of the clothes the person was wearing. The person would then be entreated to leave something for *Ndoumoi* which people usually did in sympathy for his miserable life down below. The people lived in this deception till the appointed day when the young man who had been shot was brought back to life in another elaborate hoax. It was years later that I discovered the secrets of this particular display.

Typically a magician who did this trick spent his first two weeks recruiting and training accomplices among the young men in a town. When he was confident in his accomplices, he put on the elaborate show of shooting a man in the presence of an audience. This was always an outside event that took place at night; lighting conditions would favor the magician. The gun that he used would have no bullets. Underground passages were laid in the magician's *gborji* from reasonable distances from both sides of the 'grave' where *Ndoumoi* would lie. Accomplices would watch from the entrances of these tunnels. When they saw people approaching they would observe the details of the person or group and relay it to *Ndoumoi*. Other attendants would tell *Ndoumoi* who had come and from which direction; simple but perplexing to the uninformed.

One day, several weeks after my parents had returned me to my grandfather, Uncle Jusu came home accompanied by Mama Satta. He had gone first to Malema before coming to Mano. He told me that he wanted me to go and live with him in Segbwema, which was a big town. He mentioned that he was going to send me to school where I would play with many other children and have lots of toys to play with.

"Would you like lots of toys?"

"Yes."

"What about new clothes? You will have new clothes, some for school and some for play. Would you like that?"

I nodded.

"A big lorry will take you to Segbwema. Have you sat in a lorry?"

I shook my head.

"Would you like to sit in a lorry?"

"By myself?"

"No. With Kava, your uncle."

"Yes, yes. I would like to."

"Good."

He dipped his right hand into his pocket.

"Give me your hand."

I offered my right hand as is the custom when you receive something from anyone.

"Open your palm."

I did so.

"Close your eyes."

I did so with great anticipation. In a minute or less, I felt something in my palm, something familiar but I did not quite know what.

"Now open your eyes."

I should have known. It was toffee, the type he used to give me when he first came home from the war. This one was wrapped in colourful papers.

"There will be plenty of these in Segbwema. Now go and share these with your friends."

He dispatched me with a few more toffees and I rushed to show off my treasures to my cousins and other playmates. At the end of the day, I returned to Malema with Mama Satta to await Uncle Kava. There I learnt that my going to live with Uncle Jusu was with the consent of my parents. It was not until Uncle Kava arrived four days later that my conversation with Uncle Jusu truly registered; my heart had been more on the toffees than on the promises that Uncle Jusu had made. Even then, I did not fully understand what was about to happen to me.

Chapter 2

OFF TO SCHOOL

First Lorry Ride

Diamonds were discovered in Kono District in 1931. A company, the Sierra Leone Selection Trust (SLST) was formed in 1934 to mine diamonds anywhere in Sierra Leone for a lease period of ninety nine years. From Kono, the company would need a road to take the diamonds out of the mines to Freetown and then to England. Thus began the construction of the road from Kono to the railway town Segbwema. The sixty-three mile road passed through our villages, Koilu, Moimandu, and Malema, missing Mano by a few hundred yards. The road and the increasing advantage that a cash economy bestowed on rural Sierra Leoneans also boosted their personal travel. People would use the cash obtained from trading commodities and services to pay lorry owners fares to visit other towns. It made it easier for school children to go to schools beyond the confines of their own towns and villages. It more importantly made it possible for the sick to attend the hospital in Segbwema. A journey that once took a day or two, now took only hours to complete.

The period preceding my departure for Segbwema could be described as one with days of activity and nights of apprehension. A ride in a lorry, a journey to a distant town, a life away from home; all of these generated mixed feelings in my young heart. What was it going to be like? In those days, towns and villages were like distant continents unto one another. The thirty-mile journey from my village to Segbwema was a whole-day adventure. For me, it started at dawn with great anticipation and ended at nightfall with exhaustion. On the appointed day, my mother rose up early and cooked a meal for the journey. I ate with Uncle Kava who continued to reassure me. After eating, we moved to the road to await the lorry, accompanied by an entourage of family members, well-wishers, and other curious people. As the person at the center of all this attention, I must say I basked in it with pleasure.

Other passengers were already waiting on the road when we got there. Lorries were few and far between. People could be seen straining their ears for the sound of one. Often when they thought they could hear a vehicle from a distance, it turned out to be some other sound. And so we waited in anticipation, false alert after false alert. Finally, the unmistakable sound of a lorry was heard in the distance. As the sound grew nearer, all awaiting it fixed their gaze on the bend in the road through which it would emerge. Then it appeared and was immediately greeted with commotion and excitement as passengers arranged their load for pick up. Once the passengers were all in, the lorry proceeded to the next village to deposit or pick up more people or goods. There were several such stops on the way. When we eventually arrived in Segbwema, I was too tired to show interest in my new environment. The days following could have been confusing for me but for the love and attention of my uncles.

I discovered Segbwema gradually. In the first few days after our arrival, Uncle Kava took me on a tour of the Nixon Memorial Hospital, the Methodist Hospital, as it was called then, till I knew my way around it very well. Then we ventured further into town as far as the train station. The road to the station was lined with houses on both sides, some roofed with bamboo, others with rusted corrugated iron sheets. We walked to the station a number of times. It was on my fourth visit that I saw my first train, a goods train. It did not look like anything I had imagined and was somewhat of a disappointment. It was the next day that I got real excitement when a passenger train came while we were in the station. I had never seen such a commotion that the arrival of a train could cause. My last discovery was the Methodist School which lay another mile beyond the railway. We got to the railway line, continued walking straight up a steep hill passing a large central market until we got to the Methodist School compound a mile away. The school was still closed so there were no pupils around, only workers and a few teachers. I was introduced to the head teacher, a dour looking man whose looks alone commanded good behaviour. As if sensing my unease, Uncle Kava assured me that he was not as mean as he looked. Better not be! I thought to myself.

First Day at School

On the first day of school, Uncle Kava took me to the Methodist Primary School in Segbwema. I was six years old or so. He had me enrolled as the son of Dresser Jusu, of the Methodist Hospital. Dresser was the title used for male nurses in Methodist Hospital. After enrolment, he took me to *Miisi*, the wife of the headmaster of the school and made arrangements for my lunch as the distance between the school and our house was far for me to go home for lunch. Lunch here comprised of a 'puff cake' and pepper gravy. The cake was a mixture of rice or wheat flour fried in oil. A serving was the cake split in the middle and a spoon full of pepper gravy poured in it. The headmaster's wife sold this to the pupils and teachers in the school. Everyone called her *Miisi* which I later discovered was a corruption of '*Mrs.*'

On that first day, Uncle Kava stayed to monitor events at the school, mindful of the harsh days of his own schooling and aware that I was starting school at a much younger age than he did. He left after lunch break that day which was around 11o'clock, and returned in the afternoon to accompany me home. In the weeks following, he assisted me with my schoolwork and adjustment to school life. By the time he left Segbwemafor an apprenticeship with the Sierra Leone Selection Trust Ltd. (SLST), I was happily settled into school life. The bond forged in those early years between the two of us would last a life time. When he left, the job of escorting me to and from school fell to two bigger boys in the neighbourhood. They extorted fees from me in the form of one thing or another. Mostly I gave them portions of my own meal as fee.

I completed my first school year with distinction, a fact that was communicated to Uncle Jusu via my report card and in person by the class teacher. "Dresser Jusu, Bandami's highly promising." The teacher had said. Encouraged by this initial result, Uncle Jusu embarked on building dreams for my future. He would make me a medical doctor, a person who would not have to say 'Sir' to anybody. He would forge a path to ensure that I became a doctor. This would be his life's project. In school however, I demonstrated no such ambition as my class teacher soon found out.

During an afternoon class, the teacher asked all of us pupils what occupations we would like to pursue after leaving school. As usual he began with me. I promptly replied that I would like to be a lorry (truck) driver. Disappointed, the teacher said, "You do not need a school education to be a lorry driver. With school education, you can be a teacher, a nurse, or a catechist, one who teaches about God."
I said, "I don't want to be a catechist," not even knowing what the word meant.
The teacher replied, "If you don't know what you want to be, say, you don't know."
"I don't know."
"I don't know, sir."

"I don't know, sir."

One presumptuous student asked, "Can one be a doctor?"

"Only if you are born in England," the teacher replied. Such was the geographical and cultural knowledge in those days that even to the educated protectorate teacher, England was the only place of learning and civilization. Our teacher continued around the classroom asking what each pupil wanted to be when they grew up. The two girls in the class said sensibly that they wanted to be nurses. The mission did a good job of attracting girls into nursing, a practice that locked them early into jobs with paltry remuneration and little opportunity for advancement. Boys fared better for they had a choice to be nurses, teachers, or catechists. The boys not wanting to be teachers, nurses, or catechists, and not being born in England, one by one, replied, "I don't know, sir."

In the fifties, there was little in the primary curriculum about the world outside the protectorate, beyond the three maps decorating the walls of every classroom: a map of Africa, a map of Sierra Leone showing the colony in green and the protectorate in red, and a map of ancient Palestine showing the journeys of the apostle Paul. These maps remained as abstract in our minds as the stories they told. Extracurricular activities took the form of African music and drama, and dancing. Occasionally we would learn and perform a morality play like *Everyman*, and nativity plays around Christmas. We were made to take these on the road into villages and towns at the end of the school year. These concerts served to impress the local people that their children could speak the English of the white man very well.

Jigger day

Friday at school was jigger day. It was the day of

revenge for the older boys and a day of 'wailing and gnashing of teeth' for the younger ones. Progress through the grades was performance –based, not age-based. Thus every class in the school had pupils of different ages. An age range of two to five years was not uncommon. From Monday to Friday each week, classes started with mental arithmetic. Oral problems were asked and pupils were expected to answer them promptly. If they missed, other students would be asked. If one student answered correctly, he or she was given a cane to lash all those who had missed the correct answer. It turned out that the younger ones were always better at mental arithmetic than the older boys.

In standard two, our teacher noticed a pattern involving Mary, one of the two female students, Mannah another male student, and myself. If a mental question was first posed to Mary and she got it wrong, both Mannah and I, known to be among the brightest in the class, would get it wrong if asked. Given a choice, we would rather have a lash from the teacher or other members of the class than lash Mary. The teacher moved to test our resolve in this.

One Monday morning, during mental arithmetic, he started with Mary.

"Mary, what is eight times nine?"

"Eighty four," Mary replied.

"Wrong. Mannah what is eight times nine?"

"Eighty five."

"Bandami, eight times nine?"

"Eighty six."

"You mean, you will let me or other students lash you because you don't want to lash Mary?" He asked Mannah.

"Yes, sir," Mannah replied.

"And you, Bandami?"

"Yes, sir."

"Okay, I'll teach both of you a lesson." He said, as he picked up a long cane for the exercise.

As he approached us, Mary got up and pleaded, "Please sir, beat me for both of them."

Then the class prefect stood up and begged, "Please sir, don't beat them, sir."

The teacher paused. He had never seen such solidarity among us. He decided to test the rest of the class.

"All those who do not want me to whip Mannah and Bandami, put up your hands."

Immediately the rest of the class stood up with their hands raised. Defeated, the teacher ordered a recess, and we bounced out of the classroom. This and other incidents involving Mary and Mannah forged a life-long friendship among us.

If mental arithmetic made us the young ones shine during the week, on Fridays, the tables turned against us. The last period on Fridays was hygiene. We the younger pupils were usually more careless with our hygiene as most of us had jiggers, in our toes, some all over their feet. I had colonies of them on both feet. The older boys were given the duty to clean us up. By the time they were done, several casualties would occur: many of us would be unable to walk home.

Dunwell

Dunwell had arrived in Segbwema to expand the Methodist Hospital. He was a man in his late forties and on his first visit to the African continent. He had arrived in the country with the skepticism of one who had been raised to look on Africa as primitive and Africans as heathens. He had been disabused of this view while transiting in Freetown. Many Europeans he met in the transit camp willingly shared their knowledge of the country and its people. One person he found to be particularly valuable was a Lebanese doctor who had lived and worked in Sierra Leone for many years. It was he, who had said to him,

"Unlike others, I do not dismiss all native healers as quacks. I have known remarkable results from their remedies. I remember a man with a recurring dislocation of the knee who had been treated by many doctors. Once he happened to be in the bush when it happened again, so a native medicine man was called. He applied a paste he made from various grasses and the man was cured for good. Another man was brought to me with severe inflammation of the eyes after a snake had spit into them. I gave him the standard treatment, bathed his eyes with water, put anesthetic drops in them and gave an injection of morphine but none of these methods relieved his pain. On the advice of one of my servants, he was then taken to a native healer who squeezed the juice of some herbs into his eyes. He was cured."

"Africans are not as dumb as my countrymen would have us believe, then."

"Not at all! On the contrary, if we could only respect what they know we would increase our knowledge of medicine and other practices. Our arrogance makes this impossible. Let me tell you another incident. Another patient of mine, a Lebanese trader came to me with weeping eczema on his hands and feet. He had been to many other doctors in the city but only got worse. In despair, I advised him to go to Lebanon, perhaps there, the cold weather would help. He had no intention of leaving his business behind, so he returned to the Provinces. When next I saw him, he was completely cured. He told me that a "bush" doctor had given him a paste which had cured his eczema."

"Can you obtain their knowledge and use it in your practice?" Dunwell had asked his host.

"Ah! That is the problem. The real medicine man will never disclose the secret of his medicines, not even if you offer him money. Strange, but true." His friend had responded.

Thus it was with a healthy respect for the native that Dunwell arrived in Segbwema. He was accommodated a mile across town in the Methodist School compound in a two-bedroom house, modestly furnished. He had a cook and a servant who seemed to be part of this establishment. The house and its vicinity were popular with us school children. Its compound had two of the mango trees that bore the sweetest mangoes in the town. Previous occupants were never mindful of the treasure they owned, and were never around to guard it. In mango season, it was a free-for-all. Dunwell would change all that. He preferred periodic harvests for the school. He had a fearful dog that zealously guarded the compound and was fond of chasing us for sport.

We were first filled with curiosity when he moved into his new residence. With cautious trepidation, we would approach the house to observe the reaction and behaviour of its new occupant. We soon learned that he came home for lunch at about 12 noon and that just about the time the school closed for the day, he would head to work on the construction site. Those of us who came from that part of town began to hang around hoping for a ride in his Bedford truck. He usually obliged us.

One afternoon, knowing that my playmates would not notice my absence, I went to Dunwell's compound, slipped past the dog and climbed one of the mango trees. I quickly filled my shirt with mangoes. My movements did not escape Dunwell's dog for long; soon it became so agitated that Dunwell woke up. Dunwell could not ignore the dog's insistent barking any longer and in order to get his sleep back decided to go out to the veranda to pacify him. When he failed in this, he decided to put the dog outside. Upon his release, the dog went straight to the mango tree where I was, thus revealing my presence. Dunwell went over to verify the improbable. Upon looking up the tree he saw my silhouette but could not make me out.

"Who's up there, boy? Come down this minute!" I ignored this order, by now I was shivering in my pants.

"Sit here Billy," Dunwell spoke to his dog. "Wait here till he comes down, and then hold him till I come back." He then returned to the house to resume his afternoon nap.

It was one of the marvels traded in the community that Billy would obey anything that Dunwell instructed him to do. If he said, "Chase him," Billy would chase the person out of sight and return to Dunwell. If he said, "Catch him," Billy would restrain his victim until Dunwell arrived. Everyone wondered how a dog could be trained that way.

I quickly understood my predicament. To come down would be definitely suicidal. Billy was one mean dog. He was a cross between an Alsatian and a mongrel. It stood higher than any dog in town and ran faster too. His spectacle alone aroused fear in anyone who came across him. Billy was fond of chasing schoolboys. Although he never bit them, he would leap at their shoulders from behind and wrestle them to the ground. Then he would bark at them incessantly. When the victim was thus subdued and full of fright, Billy would dart off. If this was his idea of a game, it did not amuse his victims one little bit.

As I sat pondering my dilemma, I remembered that Dunwell had to return to work. It was unlikely that he would leave his dog in that position the rest of the afternoon. I therefore decided to wait things out. Getting home late had its own consequences, but I would worry about those when the time came.

I shifted my position to be more comfortable. In doing this one mango fell out of my pocket and rolled a few yards away from the mango tree. Promptly, Billy chased it, retrieved it and returned to his post. Like lightening I saw my chance. I plucked a green mango and threw it a little farther away. Billy again promptly retrieved it and returned to his post. I climbed lower and positioned myself for a getaway. Then I threw another mango in a different direction and a little farther away. Again the dog retrieved it and sat expecting his next challenge. I inched lower and obliged, this time sending the mango downhill. As the dog chased it, I quickly descended and made my escape.

Through the grapevine, the headmaster learned of what had happened at Dunwell's house. To preempt any blame and to ingratiate himself to the school manager, he took it upon himself to identify and punish the miscreant. At assembly the following morning, the headmaster cajoled, pleaded, and threatened, but nobody knew anyone who had gone to Dunwell's compound. In the midst of his endeavour, Dunwell arrived. He encouraged the person to own up. He offered as a reward to take over the boy's education and give him all the support he would need. Nobody confessed. I was too suspicious and scared to own up.

Eventually, the truth came out. The day happened to be a Friday, hygiene day. During the week, I, as usual, had been made to lash many older boys in my class for failing at questions that I successfully answered. It was their turn to take revenge on all those who neglected their personal hygiene. I had jigger colonies covering about every part of my two feet. The older boys tended to me with passion. After the hygiene exercise I was left practically crippled. When school was dismissed I was left paralyzed with Mary and Mannah as company; Mary because she cared for me, Mannah because he cared for Mary.

After one hour, it became clear to Mary that I was not going to make it home on my own. Mary, being the bold one, thought of a way out. She would go and ask help from

Dunwell. She reached the house just as Dunwell was returning to the hospital compound after his afternoon nap. With the help of the cook and the servant, she explained her mission and asked Dunwell if he could kindly take me home.

"What about you?" He asked.

"I can walk. I will walk."

Struck by this selflessness, he offered to take us both.

"I will take both of you home."

"There is a third person." She said. "You don't have to take us all."

"Who is the third person?"

"Mannah." She replied; then added, "My friend."

"Sounds like pushing your luck, young lady. Doesn't it? But you're smart. C'mon, hop in and let's go and rescue Romeo."

He put us near him in the front seat of his Bedford truck. As we drove along, he learned our names, found out about where we lived, and we told him about various aspects of school life in Segbwema. Mary and Mannah answered every one of his questions promptly. I was in too much pain and did not contribute much to the discussion. Then Dunwell narrated the events of the previous day showing admiration for the boy who had outwitted his dog.

"Billy is a clever dog, but he was outsmarted yesterday." He said cheerfully.

No response! He dropped the subject, not knowing how to interpret our unexpected reticence.

Mary and Mannah lived in the vicinity of the hospital compound, I lived in the compound. Dunwell dropped Mary and Mannah at the hospital gate and drove me to my house. He had to carry me in his arms to the doorstep as I could still not walk. I said, "Thank you, sir."

"Not to worry, lad."

As he turned to go away, I muttered to him, "Please sir."

"Yes, son." He turned and looked at me.

"I – I – I stole the mangoes sir. I am sorry, sir."

Dunwell took a long look at me. He must have read fear in my face and must have known how difficult it must have been for me to admit my guilt. I was expecting the worst instead he smiled at me and said,

"So now we know, don't we? But don't worry. Don't let that bother you. We won't let anyone know." My fear dissipated somewhat. To reassure me further, he continued. "Listen. I come back to work about this time every day. Why don't you come to the house and wait for me so I can bring you home? Can you do that?"

"Yes, sir."

"And, the girl and the other boy can come too."

"Yes, sir."

So began an unusual friendship between an African child and an English gentleman.

The following year, Mary left for Girls School, a new school that had been established for girls four miles out of town. Mannah too left Segbwema with his parents for another town in the district. I came to rely more and more on Dunwell for friendship. With time Dunwell and I would be like father and son.

Chapter 3

RASCALS AND VICTIMS

April Fools

The bond between Dunwell and me was quickly growing. He had persuaded Uncle Jusu to allow me to go over to his house on Saturdays to do minor chores. In return, he would give me reading lessons. I was very happy with this arrangement. I would arrive and quickly do what chores there were, which was hardly any, and then settle down to read a book. Sometimes Dunwell would read to me. He taught me how to put life into my reading; how to show the writer's feelings. After reading we would do quizzes, such as what Dunwell called 'commonsense arithmetic'. It was as if Dunwell wanted to prove if the African child could think or be trained to think critically.

"Bandy, if there are ten birds on a tree and I shoot one. How many would remain?"

"On the tree?" I asked.

"Yes,"

"None."

"Why?"

"The others will fly away, sir."

"Brilliant. But how did you know?"

"My father is a hunter."

Sometimes it was moral education, and sometimes I would pose the puzzle. My own puzzles usually came from local stories I had heard from my mother. "Two thieves bragged about their expertise to each other as they traveled along a country road. They came to a bird nesting on a tree. One posed a challenge to the other. 'To show you that I am a better thief than you, I am going to steal all the eggs under that bird without it noticing.' 'Okay, do it,' said the other, accepting the challenge. One by one the first thief carefully removed ten eggs from underneath the unsuspecting bird and placed them in his own pockets. As he did this, the second equally carefully removed each egg from the other's pocket and placed it in his own. When the first thief was done, he turned to the other with satisfaction. 'See, I told you I am the better thief.' 'Okay,' said the second thief, 'but where are the eggs?' He laughed as one by one, he removed the eggs from his own pocket." At the end of the story I asked Dunwell, "Who was the better thief?"

We would reason our answers in turn and in doing so, Dunwell gained an insight into the methods of education in preliterate Mende culture.

On the first of April, people usually would try to fool others into doing something foolish unwittingly. The perpetrator then has the satisfaction of telling his or her victim, "April Fool!" On one such day, Dunwell called me and sent me on an errand. I had just arrived at his house to do my usual chores. He gave me a note to take to a Miss Cotton, one of the missionaries across town. On my way, I opened the note and read the message, "This is our April fool. Please send him to another person, and have a good laugh." I folded the note carefully, mindful of its original folds. I took the note to Miss Cotton who, following Dunwell's request, signed the note and sent me to Colonel Whitfield, the school manager on the other side of town.

I skipped this last post and went to Dunwell with a message purportedly from Miss Cotton's cook. "Miss Cotton not dere. Her cook say all white men go to Daru to practice for Governor. He say you supposed to go too."

"Of course!" Dunwell responded, startled. He could not remember the occasion, but he knew that the Governor

General was due in the region. Obviously he was supposed to be at any rehearsal. With that he thanked me and jumped into his truck and sped out of the compound to the rehearsal nine miles away. He arrived only to discover no sign of activity. He realized that he had been fooled. "Damn!" he said. "How could I be fooled by a mere brat!?" But then I was no mere brat. On his way home, Dunwell stopped to talk to Miss Cotton.

"Did Bandami come here with a note from me?"

"Yes," Miss Cotton replied. "I sent him on to Colonel as you directed. Poor boy, he must still be going all over town. I should send a note to his uncle to explain his absence, lest he gets into more trouble on his return."

Dunwell wondered whether to tell her about his rush to Daru, but on second thought decided not to make himself another joke of the day.

Farewell to a Dear Friend

I arrived early one Saturday at Dunwell's residence to learn that he was still in bed. I waited around for my orders for that day. When still Dunwell did not appear, I helped myself to a new book that I saw on his table. Then I heard,

"Call the boy."

"Yes, sir, Massah (Master)."

Thus summoned, I entered Dunwell's bedroom. It was the first time I had entered the bedroom of a white man. I was amazed at the amount of space in the room. In bed lay Dunwell. He beckoned to me.

"Come near me."

"Good morning sir."

"Good morning, Bandy. I'm afraid I don't feel good this morning. It's fever."

Malaria was the scourge of the white man. It was on

its account that Sierra Leone had been nicknamed the white man's grave.

"I am returning to England." He struggled to say. "I don't know if I will be coming back. I want you to do two things while I am gone. I am leaving the books for you." He said,referring to the shelf of children's books that he had bought for me over the years.

"I want you to read all the books that you have been reading. Read each two or three times. That is the best way to improve your English. It will also help you remember me, and our time together here."

He paused.

"Next," he continued, "the government is opening new schools in Kenema and Makeni. They are secondary schools. Kenema is a short journey by train; Makeni is farther. There is also Bo School, although admission there is currently restricted to sons and nominees of Chiefs. New opportunities are opening up for Africans like you. You should seize them. Promise me that you will not join the hospital staff or go to the Bible school. You can do better with your life, son. You can be a doctor like Dr. Johnson in the hospital here, or an administrator like the District Commissioner. You will be able to help your people if you continue with school."

By this time I had begun to understand that I was about to lose the only friend I had known since coming to Segbwema from the village. A sequence of episodes in our relationship flashed through my memory. Tears welled up in my eyes. I was confused. I felt like crying but controlled it for a while. Then it burst, the tears coming fast. I could not speak a word. I cried uncontrollably. Dunwell rose with a tremendous effort to comfort me. He held me in his arms and rocked me from side to side. We were in this position when the Sisters arrived to take Dunwell away. They looked at the scene, and then at each other: a black child and a white man in an emotive embrace in Africa.

Chapter 4

NEW HORIZONS

Train Ride

It had been several years since I first left the village to attend school thirty miles away, an unimaginable distance at the time. With time however, the distance had come to mean very little as the frequency of lorries plying the route had increased, as had the time it took to come and go. Now, to attend secondary school meant I was to go to another town much bigger than Segbwema and more than five times the distance I had ever been away from home. The only consolation was the uncle I was to live with at this new destination. Uncle Suale had come to Segbwema on annual leave and stayed with us every year the whole time I had been in Segbwema. He was fond of me and always brought gifts on those visits. The fact that I was going to live with him, together with the spirit of adventure, gave me great assurance.

The evening before my departure for Bo, Uncle Jusu and I rehearsed the journey to Bo.

"There are many stations between Segbwema and Bo. The train you are going with is the slow train. It stops at every one of these stations. The name of each station will be printed on a post. Have you seen where 'Segbwema' is printed in the station here?"

"Yes, sir."

"Every station's name will be printed like that. Look for the one that says Bo. That is where you should alight. Your Uncle Suale or someone will come and meet you in the station. Be careful." He told me.

"Tomorrow, I will buy a ticket and give it to you. The ticket is proof that you have paid your fare to travel on the train to Bo. While on board the train a man in uniform, the ticket examiner, will ask you for your ticket. At first, he will examine it, then punch a hole in it and return it to you. Keep it; don't lose it. When you are approaching Bo, he will take it from you. That is one way you will know that the next station is where you should get out." He concluded.

"Yes, sir."

"Do your best at school. Be the best that you can be. Don't fall into bad company. Uncle Suale will keep me informed about your behaviour. Don't disappoint him or me. You do well and you will get a present from me every holiday."

"Yes, sir."

"Write frequently. I would like to know how you are doing."

"Yes, sir."

The next day, Uncle Jusu went with me to the station. My entire luggage consisted of a bushel of rice and a wooden box that carried my clothes. My uncle advised me to sit on that bag of rice for in it had been concealed a cigarette cup containing my fees and pocket money. It was the first time I had been allowed pocket money, an expression of a level of confidence in my sense of responsibility that I did not miss.

The station was full of other school children returning to school from various parts of the country or making the journey for the first time, like me. Younger children were accompanied by their parents, the older ones were solo. As the train pulled out of the station, I received my final admonition.

"Write often, and be a good boy."

"Yes, sir."

He shouted other entreaties above the huff and puff of the train as it left the station. I could hardly hear him, but I could see him there on that platform waving at me until the train entered a curve and he disappeared from view. Soon after, I faced the reality of my situation; I was alone among strangers, swaying this way and that as the train raced through the terrain.

During the journey, you could tell by their confidence those who had ridden the train before; they were the ones that came down at each station and hopped onboard just as the train pulled out of the station. I sat quietly on my bag of rice, clutching my wooden box, my thoughts anybody's guess.

In Bo, after an uneventful train ride, I was met at the station by Uncle Suale and Auntie Lucy, his sister. I hadn't seen her for years. Uncle Suale hired a head-carrier to tote my bag of rice. I carried my wooden box myself. Together we trooped out of the station to my new home approximately a mile and a half away. I marveled at the houses, the number of streets, and the size of the town which spread out on all sides for as far as the eyes could see. Things seemed to be bigger here than in Segbwema. The town seemed to stretch out forever. I learnt later that Bo was the second largest town in the country with a population of around fifty thousand at the time.

Bo Town

Bo Town spread over seven hills, eight if you counted the European section of town known as 'Reservation'. It had grown from five contiguous villages that had merged into one large urban settlement. Its main roads joined in a pentagonal shape to squeeze the settlements into an inner core of similar shape and an outer one with a less defined outer geometry. Its topography and settlement pattern discouraged town planners from designing a grid system which every provincial town was intended to follow. It has continued to challenge the design of public transportation for the city to date.

Three main roads led into and out of Bo Town.

One from the west brought traffic in from and out to Freetown and the towns in between. A second road came in from the north and a third from the east. Each branched left and right as it reached into town; together they merged into the pentagonal course that formed the inner core of the town.

Before the fifties and the diamond rush, Bo Town was the largest town in the provinces. It was the main administrative town for the provinces of Sierra Leone. It boasted the largest railway station outside Freetown, a government hospital, an airstrip, and the only government secondary school in the provinces. The discovery of diamonds along the Sewa River nearby and the diamond rush of the fifties rapidly swelled its population, its commerce, and its significance. The town attracted people from the various ethnic groups in Sierra Leone and West Africa. Two new secondary schools were established, Christ the King College (CKC) by the Roman Catholics and the St. Andrew's Secondary (also known as UCC) by the United Christian Council. I had been accepted at the St. Andrew's Secondary School.

My New School

St. Andrew's was established as a central school in '54 and upgraded to a secondary school in '55. It retained a preparatory class and three regular secondary classes of forms one, two, and three, corresponding to the junior segment of a regular secondary school. I was among the pioneer students of the new secondary school. I was placed in the first form but I frequently sat in the preparatory class because most of the students there were my own age. Two were students from my previous school who had failed their Common Entrance Examination.

In response to political changes in the country, the

curriculum of schools in the protectorate had been expanded beyond literacy and religious knowledge. My new school taught French, history, nature study, geography, gardening, health science, mathematics, Latin, English language and English literature. As expected, we were taught British history and British literature with a few stories and poems from America. I loved and excelled in geography and English, both language and literature.

Papa

Uncle Suale had a great sense of humor. When he laughed it came from deep down his belly and you knew that he had given it his best. He also had a great interest in literature, an interest that intersected mine. He easily championed my interest in reading and together we explored many children's books: *Kidnapped, Round the World in Eighty Days, Treasure Island, A Tale of Two Cities*, and others. When we ran low on these he drew on his military experience in Burma.

You could never be unhappy around Uncle Suale. His approach to discipline was to inculcate initiative, promote good judgment, admit errors, own up and learn from mistakes. His academic goal for me was to help me understand what it meant to compete against myself, improve on my previous performance, self-analyze poor performance for weaknesses, and resolve to strengthen them. I was becoming to him, the son he would have liked to have at that stage in his life, an opportunity that service in the war overseas took away from him. So he lavished affection and attention on me without spoiling me. The soldier in him demanded appropriate behaviour, honesty, precision, punctuality, cleanliness, and physical fitness. He monitored my school reports regularly for evidence of these. His philosophy was 'Boys must be boys.' In dealing with my lapses, he constantly reminded himself that he too was once a school boy. So we negotiated each infraction. On many occasions it was about my report card.

"Your report says that you disrupt class on occasions. What is your explanation?"

"I don't know, sir."

"What are you going to do about it?"

"I will be quiet, sir."

"I will be looking for improvement in that area in your next report." He said, and he meant it.

Another time we explored my tardiness in school.

"Your report shows that you were late four times this term. Why was that?"

"Two times I did not finish my house work in time. The other two, my friend's leg was in a plaster. I had to help him on the way to school, sir."

Uncle Suale rewarded honesty and chastised deception. His approach was verbal rather than physical. In fact throughout our stay together, he never struck me. The open exchange with him developed my verbal facility and I became increasingly adept at explaining myself. It helped me get out of trouble in school and rationalize my actions at home, a game of deception and honesty in the two spheres of my life. Before long I came to refer to him as *Papa*, a title I retained for him till his death.

THE BULLY OF NEW GERIHUN ROAD

A new arrival in a neighbourhood always presents an affront to the boys dwelling in that neighbourhood. Thus I found myself constantly confronted by the bully of New Gerihun Road. His name was Lamijadu. He never went to school but instead spent his time harassing everyone in the neighbourhood who did, boy or girl.

I had learned from Uncle Jusu to obey and report. When Lamijadu would accost me, I would go and report to *Papa*. I did this three times before *Papa* put a stop to it. I came home one evening with another complaint.

"Lamijadu took my bucket from me at the well and would not allow me to get water." I started. "He keeps telling me that I should go back to where I came from."

"How old are you?" *Papa* asked me.

"Twelve."

"And how old is Lamijadu?"

"I don't know."

"Well, Lamijadu is twelve also. He is your equal. The next time you report Lamijadu to me, I will give you a dozen on your bare back."

I returned to the well but found that Lamijadu had thrown my bucket a little distance from the waterhole and left to cause mischief elsewhere. This in effect deferred the battle between the two of us.

Several days elapsed. Then one Saturday afternoon, I went to fetch water to launder my school uniform. I found several girls at the well. Lamijadu was there as usual holding everybody's attention by showing off his menace. Then he noticed that the girls were all gazing past him. He turned around and saw me coming towards the well, swinging my bucket and whistling a song I had learned in school that week.

"Well, well. Look who's here," Lamijadu said as I approached. "The book boy who cannot dirty his clothes. Well today, we will dirty those clothes."

The onlookers were appalled by this unfair provocation.

One of them called to Lamijadu to stop his menace. "Leave him alone," she said. "He has not done anything to you. You are always picking a fight."

Another added, "One day you will meet someone who will give you what you deserve, a good beating."

This seemed to excite Lamijadu even more. He seized my bucket and kicked it to the ground. I did not respond. He took a clump of earth and threw it at me. In a flash, I reacted. I swept him off his feet into the nearby pond. Before he could get up, I was on top of him pelting his face with blows and stuffing his mouth with dirt. The onlookers cheered as the battle progressed. I had the upper hand in this fight; I would push Lamijadu's head under the water and hold it there for a few seconds while he struggled for air. Then I would bring him up for air for a split second and put him under again. Lamijadu weakened as this continued. The commotion at the well attracted adults to the scene who recognized the potential for serious trouble. They jumped in and separated us.

"Who are your parents?" They demanded. We told them where we lived and they took us each to his own home. Lamijadu was bleeding from his mouth and from scratches on his face. His older brothers marched him to *Papa* to seek redress.

"Mr. Suale, it is your nephew. Look what he has done to our brother."

Papa referred them to the numerous times that I had come to complain about Lamijadu and the numerous times he had taken the matter up with them without satisfactory resolution. "Mr. Sesay, you used to tell me that it was a boys' game and that adults should not interfere. Let us not interfere in this case either."

Lamijadu and I became friends after that. I began teaching him the alphabet and how to write his name. I read stories to him: *Treasure Island, Kidnapped, A Christmas Carol, Tom Sawyer, Huckleberry Finn*. Lamijadu liked Huckleberry Finn. Like him, he did not have to go to school. Like Huck Finn, Lamijadu did not have strict supervision. He loved the free life. So he always made us act scenes in which he played Huckleberry Finn.

Night Raiders of Gerihun Road

Papa took up a job with the Ministry of Mines, requiring him to relocate outside Bo. Before he left, he found me a place to stay with a Mr. Fakondo, a former colleague of Uncle Jusu from Nixon Memorial Hospital. We lived a few houses from my previous residence, thus was able to maintain contact with my friend, Lamijadu. This was two years after our initial encounter. Although he had grown physically more robust, Lamijadu never challenged me again. Surprisingly, he protected me against other boys in the neighbourhood. I, in turn, never let my school knowledge get in the way of our relationship. The knowledge each of us had was to be shared with each other. Lamijadu could not do algebra but knew practical solutions to every boyhood challenge. He loved adventure and easily found a companion in me. It was he who initiated late night cooking. We would forage for condiments during the day and then take over the kitchen after the adults had gone to bed. This cooking was illicit; most of the condiments were stolen from neighbouring households. Most times we managed to get enough rice for the night. Other times when rice was not available we raided the cassava farms nearby.

Bo town was expanding, mostly in its eastern corridor, the direct effect of the diamond rush of the fifties. Speculators bought land to resell at a later date; miners did so to build their dream houses when fortune struck. Many such lands were put under cassava, potatoes, and other vegetables. As the cassava matured, they proved tempting for underfed school boys and other vagrants in the area. The owner of one of these cassava farms was a neighbour. He noticed that someone was stealing his cassava at night and immediately suspected Lamijadu and his gang. He decided to teach us a lesson.

There were five members in the Gerihun Road gang: Lamijadu, Gabriel, Abraham, and me. Gabriel and Abraham went to the CKC (Christ the King College). Unlike Lamijadu who lived with his parents and was well provided for, the three of us were always needy, of food, clothing, and other materials. Sometimes Lamijadu raided his family to support us; other times, he led us on raids in the neighbourhood. His main reward in most of it was simply adventure.

One Friday night, long after most people had gone to bed, we planned our night's escapade. Lamijadu who lived a few houses away, had during the day acquired some meat from the slaughterhouse. He now brought it with the decaying smell in his wake. Gabriel and Abraham would go for the cassava. I was to steal a chicken. I quickly accomplished that. Lamijadu and I proceeded to make the fire to prepare the chicken against the arrival of Gabriel and Abraham. Soon, everything was ready and we told each other stories as we waited. Then we heard a loud bang! Then another!

We got up. We looked around. Nothing stirred. We had just sat back down in front of the fire when Gabriel and Abraham came rushing in. Gabriel collapsed on the floor moaning, "I'm shot! I'm shot! O-o-o I'm dying." He was soon joined by Abraham, also writhing in pain. They both rolled over and over as they moaned. We were all shocked. We held them down and examined each. There was no blood on their bodies. We kept asking, "Where? Where?" "We cannot see the blood." We sat them up as their breathing slowed down. Each felt his body, this way and that. A sense of realization seemed to sink in. Danger was not imminent. Then we heard a cough nearby; someone was approaching us in the dark. A human form materialized gradually, first the feet and the robe came into view, then the face of a man. Alas, a familiar face: Kothor Barrie, our neighbour. He had a broad smile on his face. Now, he stood over us. Then we recognized the gun in his right hand.

"*Pipul den we de tiff me cassada, ar don ketch den tiday* (Those who have been stealing my cassava, I have caught them today.)"

We looked at him and said nothing. Then he knelt down and sat by us. He narrated his own life when he was in *marabou* school learning the Quran. He recounted how often he went to bed hungry; how often they had to beg in the town so they could eat. He taught us about how God looked on the kind of stealing that we were engaged in saying that there is no *haram* (sin).

"Haram comes from greed," He said, "When you steal in order to profit from it, not when you do it to support a life."

At the end of the lecture, he asked me to go with him to his house. Once there, he asked his wives to give me a bowl of rice to take back. We were grateful but such spoils were never as good as those obtained from plunder. So for the second time that evening, I raided our house for a few cups of rice which I carried in my trouser pockets. We still had an enjoyable evening but we never raided Kothor Barrie's cassava farm again.

KINDO THE ROBBER

For many schoolboys who had come to Bo Town to attend St Andrew's or CKC, it was common practice to fetch firewood from the forest or nearby farms for their guardians. Usually the boys would do it in groups, occasionally alone. On one fateful Saturday, I needed to get firewood for my home but I could find no other boy ready to fetch firewood that day. Lamijadu had found a more exciting adventure in watching a football match. As my guardian desperately needed firewood, I ventured out alone. I went past one village and turned into a bush not far from that village. This was a familiar place for fetching firewood. I had only gone half a mile from the main road when I came upon a stream and a group of men gathered in a circle. When they saw me, they all rose in a menacing manner.

"Who are you?"

"What do you want?"

"Where are you going?"

"Where are you from?"

The questions came fast and from many directions. I was scared! Then one man raised his hand and signaled to them to sit down. Then he beckoned to me to approach him. I could not. My impulse was to run, but my feet betrayed me.

"Come. Don't be afraid. Nobody is going to hurt you."

Still I could not move. I am sure by that time I was trembling all over. Was I dreaming? Was I on Treasure Island? Were these pirates? I tried to move forward, but I could not. Then the man, who must have been the leader of this gang, rose up and slowly approached me. He laid his hands around my shoulder and pulled me to his side such that my head came to rest on the left side of his chest. With his right hand, he rubbed my head.

"Boy, what is your name?"

"Bandami."

"Where do you come from?"

"Gerihun Road, sir."

"I mean, 'Where is your home?'"

"Segbwema, sir."

"Is that where your parents live?"

"Yes, sir."

"How long have you been in Bo?"

"One year, sir."

"Do you know me?"

"No, sir."

"What is my name?"

"I don't know, sir."

"Where do I live?"

"I don't know, sir."

"What are you doing here?"

"I came to get firewood."

"Alright, sit down here and these men will help you."

He ordered the men to gather firewood for me. Then he took a loaf of bread, stuffed it with corned beef, and gave it to me.

"Which school do you go to?"

"St. Andrew's."

"Recite a poem for me."

I recited *The Ballad of Dick Turpin,* a poem I had recently studied. As I did this, I lost my fright; I recited with great animation. The man was clearly impressed with my performance. By the time I was finished, the gang had put together a bundle of firewood for me. They put it on my head and they all wished me goodbye. As I left, the leader handed me a three-penny piece and said, "Here, this is for lunch tomorrow. And thanks for the poem. Oh, and if anyone asks you if you saw us, say you did not. Understand?"

"Yes, sir. Thank you, sir."

I left, thankful to the group for helping me get firewood. It was more than what I would normally have fetched on my own but I would manage to get home with it, labor as I did under it. When I got to Fagoyah village, I met a group of men deliberating with an old woman who pointed to me as I approached them. She had observed me go along the road toward the *Kendeyama* stream where, it was rumored, the Kindo gang had been hiding out. I decided to rest here for a short while and put my load down. A man confirmed to the group that he had seen Kindo's gang go in that direction that morning. It turned out that they had been planning a rescue mission when I appeared. They had thought that I might be in danger. The chief asked if I had seen anybody and I said 'no'. The old woman asked how I had got my wood so quickly. I replied that I had hidden most of it on an earlier mission. After resting, I resumed my journey home, this time with the knowledge and fear of a murderous gang propelling me. I never fetched firewood in that area for the rest of my stay in Bo Town.

This incident came at the end of my third year at St. Andrew's Secondary School in Bo. The school's management decided at the end of that academic year, not to add the senior forms (grades) to the school as had been planned. Students were encouraged to seek admission in other schools. Bo School had opened its doors to students other than sons and nominees of paramount chiefs. I took an entrance examination for the school and was admitted into form three.

Chapter 5

BO SCHOOL

Greener

When Bo School was established by the British in 1906, it was patterned after its public schools. It was the "Eaton of West Africa." At its inception, its main object was to train the sons of chiefs "in such a manner as to make them good and useful rulers of the country in the future."

The compound was divided into three sections: the dormitory area, the recreation area, and the classroom area known as 'up the school'. It was a large compound, fenced in on all sides. Two gates served to enter and leave it. The one on the eastern side was the main gate. Taking a left turn took one to the electricity department, the public works department, the hospital, and further on to the police station and the northern part of Bo Town. A right turn from this gate took one to the post office, the railway station and the rest of Bo Town. The gate on the southern side was less frequently used. It led out to the station, the staff quarters, and the outskirts of Bo Town.

By 1960, the school's population had increased to three hundred and sixty odd students living in four dormitories named after towns: Paris, London, Manchester, and Liverpool. (Manchester was originally Berlin; it was renamed during World War I.) The dormitories were self-contained two-storey buildings with four open chambers with beds arranged in two opposite rows, twenty two per chamber. It had cubicles attached to each chamber for prefects. A storage room underneath the stairs was converted to a study and dubbed 'the dungeon'. On admission, a student was assigned to a 'town'. I was admitted into Paris. The school was in effect a self-contained 'settlement' with restrictions on leaving and entering for its residents. For me, having lived in Bo Town for three years, there were enough attractions outside those walls that frequently beckoned to me. That got me into trouble from time to time.

Life in Bo School started with a formal induction into the school's culture in an elaborate ceremony that started with a parade of newcomers around town. This was referred to as the *greeners' parade* and it signaled to the town that a new cycle had begun in the school. It was an annual carnival for the town as the new comers, embellished with green leaves, jogged through town.

Beginning from the dining hall, two rows of 'greeners' jogged through the southern gate, turning right and east toward the staff quarters. They were accompanied by older and more senior students who maintained order in the ranks. The leader turned left a few hundred yards from the gate onto the main road that brought motor traffic from Freetown, and turned left into Bo Town. They jogged non-stop through Tikonko Road, turned right into Prince Williams Street, and continued for a mile, to a roundabout at the top of a hill. Then the line snaked left on MaheiBoima Road for another mile, then Kissi Town Road, Hospital Road, Dambara Road and back to the compound. In all, it covered a distance of five miles and was conducted non-stop. Onlookers cheered them along offering drinks of water and soda to the weary. The ceremony ended in the evening with drama and literary flourish in the dining hall, complete with a master of ceremony. It was designed to impress academic excellence upon the initiates and to instill a sense of loyalty to the school.

When I entered the school, its principal was W. D. Smith, M.A (Oxon) a Scottish gentleman who had served in the British civil service in India. He was in the last days of his service and patience was not one of his virtues. To put it mildly, he was unreasonable; he easily snapped at anything and everything. His memory however was phenomenal. As part of his duties, he collected the sports fund each year. Once he had received a pupil's sports fees and assigned an admission number to him, he remembered that pupil's name and number for life. This was a fact little known to new comers, and one that I found out to my dismay one day.

AMIGO AND THE FIGHT FOR THE CLASS BUCKET

Once admitted, transfer students met with stiff competition in their new classes. Bo School boys studied very hard. The school was academically the best in the country and every student felt a responsibility for maintaining that status. The classes were so competitive that it took an exceptionally brilliant student to repeat the same academic position in an academic year. The school year was divided into three terms, each ending with a class exam. The end of year exam was the determining one; it ascertained those who would be promoted, those who would repeat the class, and those who would be expelled from the school altogether.

Amigo was my classmate. We lived in the same dormitory too. He liked to bully and intimidate new comers. During our first prep evening, Amigo interrupted everybody with an 'important announcement'. "Gentlemen, behold the *class bucket*(bottom of the class) of the year."

"Who?"

"Bandami."

The class giggled until a prefect stopped by to hush everyone up. My intimidation and harassment by Amigo did not end there. He continued even in the dormitories. If he found me studying, he would say to me, 'Why are you wasting your time? You are already the class bucket. Do you honestly believe that you can come from a *kwekwe* school like St. Andrew's and beat anyone in that class? Stop dreaming."

I began to believe Amigo and gave in to him. My study efforts waned as did my homework activities. This continued till the end of the first term and into the examinations. We returned to class the following term only to learn that while I had come fourteenth in my class, Amigo had come twenty eighth! I laughed to myself and chastised myself for falling prey so easily to Amigo's mischief. Thereafter, I was in the first five in all academic activities in my class and ended the year in the second position while Amigo failed and dropped out of school.

The quality of one's life in Bo School was shaped by the friends that one cultivated. I should say the *gang* one socialized in. Weeks after my initiation, I found myself associating with three other students with whom I shared a common interest. We read voraciously. We became so well known in the local bookshop, that if a new novel arrived, a copy was kept for us. Sometimes it was even bought for us by the bookshop staff. Initially, we lived in separate dormitories. By the end of our time in Bo School, we had moved together into London Block C.

As a gang, we assumed aliases after characters in our novels. I was Lemmy Caution, after Peter Cheyney's lead detective. Another person was Poirot, after Agatha Christie's. Then there was Sherlock Holmes, from Sir Arthur Conan Doyle, and Slim Callaghan, another Cheyney character. In our pastime, we played detectives in make believe scenarios. Although we took different paths in life after Bo School, our friendship has endured.

Teachers

We had an interesting cast of teachers in the school during my stay. Each had something that distinguished him. There was Mr. Johnson with the terrible lisp. When he said 'exercise thirty-three,' you heard 'epper pie pappy pree.' He was a father to my form three class. Never mad at any of our jokes and pranks; always advising us to study hard for a secure future.

There was Mr. Sogbandi, the flamboyant, ostentatious, and intimidating teacher; the, 'only Kono man with a BA degree.' He was the colourful referee of Bo Town's soccer matches. He was the referee who accompanied every whistle he blew with a demonstration of the infringement. He always intimidated us with threats like, "I will sit on you with double energy." He taught history with gusto. In our revenge, we nicknamed him 'Amboyna' after the Amboyna massacre, one of his favorite topics in our British Empire history textbook.

There was Mr. Sanders our Latin teacher, who always wore Khaki shirts and trousers. He was a Sierra Leonean who had lived most of his life in Ghana. Legend had it that he had been a journalist in Ghana. We dubbed him 'SOS' and teased him for not being able to speak any Sierra Leonean language. We teased him often for his love for roasted groundnuts and his tendency to speak in between pops of his delight. We teased him also for the khaki suit he always wore. The diamond rush of the fifties produced a generation of students who turned up in school with better clothes than some of their teachers, especially 'SOS'.

There were teachers that we loved. Like another Mr. Johnson our second math teacher. He was an old boy and always behaved as if he was still a school boy. He was closer to our social lives than any of the other teachers. He organized our quizzes; he conducted our choir; he instituted community hymn singing; he was our soccer coach; he was our scoutmaster also. We loved and trusted him so.

Then there was Mr. Conton (later principal) who taught us history and English in form five after Mr. A.B. Gembeh and Mr. Glen Caulker died, the former in a car accident, the latter mysteriously. Conton had published *The African* which distinguished him among the staff. He was our pride and we always dared pupils from other schools to show us a person like him on their staff.

Our chemistry teacher was the one with the four to five syllable English words. He had left Sierra Leone to study medicine and returned with a bachelor degree and a healthy command of big words. We would wear studded shoes that caused a noise on the cement floor as we walked just to provoke him, and he would admonish us not to be 'ostentatious.'

There was Teacher Sesay who had been brought from an elementary school. He had a serious challenge with the Queen's English. He would say ungrammatical sentences and when challenged, would cite a grammatical rule as authority for what he said. He also taught us history. He would ask, "When did the American colonies revolted?" The class would burst out laughing and he would say, "Past participle, past participle." We had to learn to separate his knowledge of history from his erroneous utterances.

Prefects

Prefects formed the second tier of authority in Bo School. In general, senior boys lorded it over junior boys. A *magbevi* (a hard knock on the head) from a senior boy was a common experience among junior boys in forms one to three. I got mine for the first time while innocently visiting a prefect for homework help. The person who delivered the knock had nothing to do with my visit and the code of behaviour was such that my host could do nothing on my behalf.

One soon learnt to avoid oppressive seniors or hoped for opportunities for clandestine revenge against them. My revenge against my first bully came one Saturday evening when I was approached by a timid female figure entering the gate by the Paris dormitory. She beckoned to me and I went to meet her. She carried a basket. She asked if I knew Sule Kamara in Manchester Block B. I said I knew him very well. She asked if I could convey her basket to him. I readily said yes and asked if she was going to wait for an answer.

"*Nar chop. Lehee send the pan bak* (It is food. Let him return the dishes)."

I vanished into the darkness. I summoned my friends to the laundry where we demolished the food. We washed the dishes and packed them neatly into the basket, allowed a decent time to elapse, then I took the basket back to her.

"*Wetinee say* (What did he say)?"

"He said to say thank you. That he is busy with his classmates on a project and that he will see you later tonight or tomorrow morning."

She left with satisfaction oblivious of the plot she had fallen prey to. The secret never leaked. Sule found out later but could do nothing about it. For one, it was forbidden for him to entertain female visitors on campus. Also, out of three hundred and sixty boys in the school he could not determine who the culprit or culprits could be. Such was life.

One of the functions of prefects was to monitor our movement on campus, especially after school. The roll was called twice a day; at 4 o'clock and 10 o'clock, to check for who was on campus and who was not. Skillful bound breakers always worked their activities around these events. One way to circumvent it was to have a colleague answer for you when you were not going to make it to a roll call. Sometimes it worked, sometimes it didn't. It did not work when a perceptive prefect had been forewarned of an absence or had detected a quiver in a responding voice. In both cases, he would pause and repeat the name while directly looking in the direction of the last response. At that point the impostor would chicken and the prefect would record the absence.

Bound breaking was always punishable, usually by being given a military drill or equivalent punishment. It never deterred the hardened bound breakers. Vassimu, a classmate of mine would always say, "Why should you be caught?"

We had ingenious ways of avoiding detection when we broke bounds. Sometimes we used disguises. Once, three of us escaped detection from two prefects by pretending to be drunkards walking the street. We went right past them and they did not recognize us. We would also use such means to go to the movies, especially on weekends.

In the last quarter of his service as principal of Bo School, Pa Smith felt that discipline was declining in the school. He felt he had to clean up before his successor took over from him. He ordered the prefects to report all cases of misbehaviour to him directly. One weekend, there was a bash at Demby Hotel. Some of my classmates attended it. I sneaked out too, but went to a *fufule bar*, a local outlet, in New Site. The big attraction was to dance the rock and roll. On my way back to campus I passed by Demby Hotel. I ran into a 'policeman' who advised me not to linger around.

"Go straight to campus. Anyone caught out this night is going to be expelled."

I did not need persuasion to hurry back to campus. While in the dormitory, I could hear the names of some classmates coming over the PA system. They were in dancing competitions oblivious of the scouts monitoring their conduct outside the hall.

By noon the following Sunday a grim picture had emerged of the number of boys who had been identified at Demby's.

First my concern was for a town mate of mine whose name was on the list. He was so distraught, he could not eat breakfast and lunch. I tried to spare him from being expelled. After the 1 o'clock roll call, it became clear that his name was on the list and that he would be facing the principal the following morning. I assured him that I would do what I could to save him.

"What can you do?"

"Remove your name from the list."

"Not possible. If you do that I promise you …."

"Consider it done."

I stole a master key from a friend and waited till the Senior Prefect had left the dormitory. I quickly entered his cubicle, found my friend's name and simply ran a pen through it the way other names had been scratched out. At 4 o'clock the final list was called out, and my friend's name was not among them. I have remained in his gratitude till this day.

After the 4 o'clock roll call, the gravity of the situation hit home. A significant number of those on the list to be presented to the principal in the morning were from my class. Classmates agreed that the situation was not tenable. We were to do something to avert disaster, but what? My gang, the Lemmy Caution gang as we called ourselves, withdrew to a safe spot out of site. First, we swore our usual oath of allegiance. Then, we brainstormed the situation.

"What can we do?"

"We can tear the relevant pages from the punishment book."

"No. The prefect will suspect us, the usual suspects of misdemeanor."

"The only way to avoid disaster is to make the punishment book disappear."

"Yes, but how."

We brainstormed the how for a few minutes. We hatched a plot in which we would use a master key and enter the prefect's cubicle and steal the punishment book. We would then find a way and send it up the manhole in the ceiling of our toilet on the upper floor of Paris block. Our plan succeeded. I would not be surprised if that book is still lodged up the ceiling of Paris blocks A and B. Upon discovery of the loss, the prefect ordered simultaneous searches of all the dormitories yielding nothing. In the days following, he looked at me with suspicion but could never tie me to the act. Thus a disaster for our class was averted.

Policemen

Below the rank of prefects were policemen, and just like a regular police force, they ranged in rank from an ordinary policeman to commissioner. These were appointed from the senior segment of the school, usually form four, by the Senior Prefect at the beginning of each academic year. Policemen supervised the prefects' prescriptions for punishment, which were usually in the form of military drills. On Saturdays they added 'sanitary fatigue' which was a term for cleaning tasks around campus. During the week, the prefects would record names of people who committed various offenses. After lunch on Saturdays, the whole school was summoned by the dining hall bell for roll call. After roll call, the punishment book would be read out and pupils exited the dining hall as their names were called. Thereafter, pupils without punishment obligations were free to go to Bo Town as long as they were back when the next roll was called. Inspector Massaquoi

Isaiah Massaquoi was a police commissioner, a tall athletic young man with a 'no nonsense' look. He was as strict as he was unreasonable. In our books, he was just mean. He was not easy to befriend. I first fell foul with him over my *kpoki* (a blend of groundnut paste and rice flour with sugar to taste) when I arrived in school in the second term of my first year.

It was the practice among senior boys to deprive junior boys of snacks their parents had prepared for them during the holidays. They would plot to explore what each junior boy had brought from the holidays. One common strategy was to order 'box inspection' on one pretext or another. That way, they would discover who had what in his box. I had fallen prey to this practice in my first term and sworn it would not happen to me again.

One day, after the inspection, I took my *kpoki* across campus and lodged it with *Kortor* (or *Ngoh*: meaning 'elder brother' -the titles used for senior boys) Baimba, a senior friend in Manchester who was a prefect. This friend was known to my parents and had offered to look after me in Bo School. When Commissioner Massaquoi demanded my *kpokie*, I told him where it was. When he ordered that I retrieve it, I refused. This annoyed him. The following Saturday he attempted to punish me. I resisted and took my case to the senior prefect and won. Thereafter there was no love lost between him and me. I knew it would be a matter of time before he sought his revenge.

There was a gutter by Liverpool that was called Lamu. It ran from the kitchen through the laundry and emptied into a swamp by the swimming pool. Other drainage gutters from Paris, Manchester, London, and Liverpool itself discharged into it. It was the dirtiest gutter on campus. One Saturday, three weeks after our last confrontation, I was called out after the 1 o'clock roll call for punishment because I had 'broken bounds' (left campus without permission) that week. Commissioner Massaquoi saw his opportunity for revenge. He ordered a group of us to clean Lamu. He even insisted that we clean this gutter with our bare hands. We refused. He vowed to march us to the senior prefect in the evening. He left and went to town. In his absence, we rallied friends and cleaned the gutter with shovels, sticks, and hoes. I am sure Lamu had never been so clean and never was after our effort.

True to his word, Commissioner Massaquoi, marched us to the senior prefect and made his case against us. We challenged his account of events and gave an embellished narrative of our own, concluding with an allegation of malice. "These boys refused to carry out their punishment."

"Is that so? Did you boys refuse punishment?"

"No sir. We did our punishment. He just hates us. He asked us to clean Lamu gutter with our hands and we did. He said that we did not clean it properly. We told him that we were going to report him for putting our health at risk. He said he would see about that!"

"Now boys, this is serious. Are you sure you cleaned the gutter as you were told?"

"Yes, Prefect. Go and see for yourself."

We all walked to Lamu gutter with the senior prefect. We suppressed our laughter at the shocked look on Massaquoi's face when he saw the gutter. The prefect was not amused.

"NdakeiMassaquoi, how well did you expect the boys to clean this gutter. It is a gutter, for goodness sake. You should not take advantage of boys. I think I need to set an example here."

Massaquoi was demoted from commissioner to inspector for two weeks and admonished to be fair in his dealings with offenders. He never bothered me again.

Kondor Managers

Another tier of authority below that of prefect but at par with policemen was that of *Kondor Managers*. *Kondor* is a popular term for food served in public institutions. It is notoriously unlike home food and takes getting used to. That taste once acquired never leaves the individual. In Bo School, *kondor* managers supervised the distribution of the food once it had left the kitchen. It was their duty to ensure that the prefects and senior boys got the best part of the food and that no one 'doubled', that is, ate a share in addition to his own. As it was, doubling was endemic in the school, especially among junior boys whose rations were never enough for their active stomachs.

We adopted ingenious ways to create opportunities to 'double.' One of them was to create the impression that a table was full or had enough occupants at the beginning of the school term when dining seats were assigned. That way there was always an extra plate or two on the table. We developed catch phrases to warn of the presence of a *kondor* manager. One such phrase was C-A-P; A-I-C which stood for 'Cut and pass; Amadu is coming' where Amadu was the manager in the vicinity. Doubling was usually punishable.

Kondor had a yearning effect on the Bo School boy. Even when we went to town and returned with full stomachs we would still answer the *kondor* bell for dinner. With lame excuses we would claim to be going 'just to eat my meat' and end up emptying our plates. Such was the hold *kondor* had over us.

KONDOR PROGRESSIVE UNION (KPU)

Another way students circumvented doubling, was to join the *Kondor Progressive Union* (KPU). The KPU club was a notorious organization on campus. This coterie of gormandizers had the exclusive right of doubling food rations without incurring punishment. To qualify for membership, one had to eat four regular plates of rice, four loaves of bread, and four bananas. Initiation into this exclusive club was once a term; it was conducted by *Kondor* managers. Once admitted, one remained a member throughout his Bo School days.

There were many interesting stories about membership failures and successes. Some were daunting, others simply hilarious. Take the membership of Sengbe who had eaten four plates of rice, four loaves of bread and four bananas. Well, almost four bananas. For after swallowing the last piece of the fourth banana, there had been a loud 'pop' and Sengbe had vomited it all. Variations on this story include the detail that he had farted before vomiting, or that he had vomited then farted. Anyway, the panel concluded that since he had swallowed the last piece of the banana before vomiting, he had in effect eaten it. He therefore qualified for membership. For this performance we dubbed him "Four-Four-Four."

Chapter 6

PREFECT MANNAH

This Boy is Dangerous

Prefect Mannah was another senior with whom I had many encounters. He was reputed to be the most unreasonable authority on campus, but in my scrapes with him, I always managed to outwit him. On a certain day when he was on duty, I showed up in line with one of those shorts that he had unilaterally vowed to outlaw. It was a new style that was creeping into vogue: flared short pants that carried a buckle at the back. We called them 'zoot pants'. Prefects just hated it. That afternoon, when Prefect Mannah spotted me wearing these 'zoot pants', he decided to match me up to the principal.

"Bandami, get out of my line. Go up the school and wait for me by the principal's office. I said by the principal's office."

I had learnt long ago not to argue with authority, more so a prefect. It simply made matters worse. So, I got out of the line and proceeded to the Principal Smith's office.

Now it was common knowledge that in Pa Smith's court, he that first made a report eventually won his case. So when Prefect Mannah told me to go and wait for him at the principal's office, it was a decision that he would, forever, regret. I quickly walked up to the principal's office and, without waiting for Prefect Mannah, knocked on the door and, when told to enter, went in.

"1XX3 Senessie, what can I do for you, boy?" Pa Smith asked me in his strong nasal voice.

"Prefect Mannah said I should come and report myself to you sir."

"Well, what have you done this time?"

"Nothing, sir. He just hates me. Today he said that I am not in uniform and that I should come and report myself to you, that I am not in uniform."

"Well, I see you wearing a white shirt and a pair of khaki shorts. I believe that is the uniform of the school. Look, enough of this nonsense. Go back to him and tell him that I say your uniform is alright."

"Yes, sir. But he is not going to be satisfied with that sir. He has threatened to have me expelled sir." I lied.

"Oh, you run along boy. It will be alright."

"Yes, sir. Good day, sir. Have a nice day, sir."

I came out of the Principal's office and stood outside as if I had been waiting there the whole time. Along came Prefect Mannah confident that he was going to teach me a lesson. "Follow me," he said gruffly. I followed him, looking as hopeless as a lost cause. As we entered the office, the Principal rose to meet us. His mood was as foul as Prefect Mannah or anybody had ever encountered. Before Prefect Mannah could speak, Pa Smith forestalled him.

"No, no, no, Mannah! You are silly! You are stupid! Leave this wretched boy alone! Leave my office! Leave my office! I don't want to see you! I don't like to see senior boys picking on junior boys. I won't have that."

Prefect Mannah was too stunned to do anything. With his right hand the old man turned him around, pushed him out of the office and closed the door after us. I was still in a daze when I got to my own class. Not being one to gloat over my luck, I said nothing about this episode to my classmates when they inquired about what had happened. I simply told them that I had apologized to Prefect Mannah. So, this little episode remained a secret between Prefect Mannah and me. The following week, when Prefect Sandy wanted to march me up for the same reason, it was Prefect Mannah who cautioned him against it without offering reasons. He simply said, "If I were you I wouldn't do that, Sandy. This boy is dangerous." Prefect Sandy understood from this caution that Prefect Mannah was signaling his protection for me. So the word spread among Prefects that I was under Prefect Mannah's protection and should not be touched.

The Case of the Missing Grape Fruit

Where structures did not exist to beat the system, one devised ingenious ways to outsmart its agents. My second scrape with Prefect Mannah followed hard on the heels of the first. The fruits on campus were forbidden. Anybody caught plucking them would be severely punished. If he was lucky, he could be drilled till he collapsed. If he was not, he could be suspended; worse still expelled. This rule was so strictly enforced that law-abiding pupils would walk away from a windfall. Not so, the more adventurous. For them the condition "if you were caught" presented the challenge in the form of, "Why should I be caught?" I was always drawn to such challenges.

One such occasion came during the midterm break in the third term of the school year. The mid-term break had been announced. Those who wished to spend the holiday weekend could obtain *exeats* (permission slips) and leave the campus. I had been invited to Freetown by an uncle, and a benevolent benefactor had offered me a return train ticket to Freetown. I applied for, and obtained, an *exeat* to go to Freetown.

Prefect Mannahremained suspicious of my activities although he had no evidence to support his suspicions. So, out of frustration, he summoned me one evening to register his reservations. "Every trouble in this school has something to do with you. If you are not at the center, you still have something to do with it. Yet you look so innocent. Well, let me tell you this. You don't fool me. In fact I am on the lookout for you. The day I catch you, you will leave this school. So reform yourself or start packing your box."

"Prefect I beg. I swear I have nothing to do with anything. Whoever told you that is telling lies. I swear."

"Well, we'll see. But remember, I mean it."

"Yes, Prefect."

Prefects were so powerful that they could effect the expulsion of a student by merely recommending it to the principal. The very next day, I would fall into Prefect Mannah's net, well almost.

It was a Thursday, the day when the mid-term holiday was declared. A classmate and I had skipped morning school and gone to steal grapefruits to take home for the mid-term. The trees were between our dormitories: Paris, and London. Illicit harvesting was forbidden and strictly punishable. Unexpectedly, Prefect Mannah came down from up campus while school was still in session. He thought he saw someone harvesting grapefruits and plotted to catch him in the act. When he finally made his move, his quarry was gone. In disappointment he returned to the dormitory. On impulse, he decided to check upstairs in the Paris Block to see if anyone was hiding there. He saw no one in the dormitory, but his search was richly rewarded. He found a travelling bag full of grapefruits.

"Well," he must have said to himself, "Take the bag and you will find the man behind the bag." So he took the bag and locked it up in his cubicle. He was happy and excited that finally the miscreant he had been waiting to apprehend all this while was about to be caught. To prolong the agony of his victim, he would defer the resolution of this matter until the end of the school day.

From my hiding place I heard the locking of doors

and concluded that Prefect Mannah was leaving. I crawled out to a safe distance and peeped out to check. There in the distance I could see the straight but retreating figure of Prefect Mannah walking gingerly to school. I beckoned to my friend that the coast was clear. We came out of hiding to find the bag of grapefruits gone. We easily concluded that it was Prefect Mannah who had taken it. This brought on additional worries particularly for my friend who owned the bag. Once out of hiding, we began to quarrel.

My friend Kebbie was in torment. What if he went to claim the bag? He would have to admit that it belonged to him. Prefect Mannah would find him guilty of not just stealing the grapefruits but doing so during school hours. He could be suspended or expelled. How would he explain this to his parents? He should never have listened to me. Kebbie confronted me.

"It is all your fault!" he said as he came down the stairs. "I did not want to be involved in this. You said it would be alright. Now see what you got me into."

I was thinking hard. I had suspected that Prefect Mannah had locked the bag up in his cubicle. Not wanting Kebbie to follow me, I told him to stay upstairs and be on the lookout while I continued to search for the bag. Working quickly, my heart thumping, I opened the cubicle with the master key I had now become accustomed to getting from my friend George whenever the need arose. Quietly, I emptied the bag of grapefruits on the floor and carefully locked the door when I was done. I then returned the key and closed the dormitory after me. I heard Kebbie descending the stairs still bitterly complaining about the predicament I had put him in. I concealed the bag as I waited for him to reach me. As he approached, I took out the bag and thrust it in his face with contempt.

"Now stop whining, you coward! Here is your bag, *maadada*

(cry baby). But remember this. If Prefect Mannah returns and finds it with you, I never saw it, and I don't know anything about today. May God help you."

Without civility we parted company. I returned to class as if nothing had happened. Later that day I caught the train to Freetown for my mid-term holidays.

By his own account, Prefect Mannah stayed 'up the school' after school to prolong the agony of his victim. In his mind, whoever it was would need his bag to travel. He would make sure that that person did not travel that day. When he felt it was too late for anyone travelling by train or lorry to do so, he returned to the dormitory. With a sense of fulfillment he proceeded to his cubicle to retrieve the travel bag. As he opened the door he saw the grapefruits rolling all over the floor in front of him. He was shocked and disappointed. He slumped into his chair gazing at the floor. He sat like that for a long time wondering what to do. Who could it be? There could be only one answer: Bandami! "But I can't prove it." He said to himself. "You have to give it to him. I am afraid that boy will make a criminal one day." He prophesied. He realized that he was no longer angry. His anger had been transformed into admiration and amusement.

By the time I returned to school on Tuesday the following week, Prefect Mannah had not only forgotten the matter, he had forgiven me. He had begun to admire the smoothness of my operations. In his reckoning, I had become a celebrity. To more unfortunate miscreants in the future he would say, "You fellows should learn from Bandami. He uses his brains." Or, "You boys are so stupid. Why don't you ask Bandami for advice?" But even though he remained convinced that it was I that had pulled this trick on him he never got me to admit it. This irritated him somewhat. It was to become a game the two of us would fondly play all through our adult lives.

Chapter 7

THE BROTHERHOOD

Bonding

WHILE SOME OF THE ESCAPADES DESCRIBED IN PRECEDING CHAPTERS WERE IN THE NAME OF GETTING BACK AT OVERBEARING AUTHORITY FIGURES, THEY WERE ALSO PART OF BEING A BO SCHOOL BOY. THE INSTINCT FOR SURVIVAL DROVE ONE TO CONFRONT CHALLENGES WITH INGENIOUS MEANS. BUT BO SCHOOL WAS MORE THAN THAT. IT WAS ABOUT SUCCESS, ACADEMIC SUCCESS; IT WAS ABOUT FORGING A BROTHERHOOD. IT FORGED BONDS ACROSS ETHNIC BOUNDARIES, BONDS THAT WOULD LAST A LIFETIME, MARKED BY LOYALTY AND COMMITMENT TO FELLOW BO SCHOOL BOYS. OCCASIONALLY, ROGUE ELEMENTS TESTED SUCH TIES; USUALLY THEY WERE IDENTIFIED AND WEEDED OUT. SUCH CIRCUMSTANCES ALSO SERVED TO STRENGTHEN TIES FOR THOSE WHO SURVIVED SUCH CHALLENGES. THIS BROTHERHOOD WAS FORGED IN MANY CRUCIBLES, AND IT TOOK MANY FORMS.

The Immaculate Four

Whenever Bo School boys left the confines of their compound, they felt and behaved as if they were on a stage and were being observed by all. Bo Town for them was their audience and they dressed and performed to satisfy. The pupils who epitomized this the most were the Immaculate Four. They were a band of Bo School brothers that hung out together. On outing days, they went to town together and returned together. They dressed immaculately: white *terylene* shirts with executive tergal or gabardine-wool grey pants. The most notable of them was Okulele. They set the standards for others to follow. If they got caught in the rain, they would walk leisurely through it without any outward sign of discomfort. Before long, you would not catch a Bo School boy running from the rain, the message being that there was more clothing waiting in the box.

One day, the quartet sneaked into a matinee dance at Demby's Hotel. There was a back-to-school dance organized by CKC boys. The four arrived at the hall, bought their tickets and entered. They scouted out for four girls and invited them to dance. These were the days of the waltz, the tango, and the highlife, and the Immaculate Four could do any of these dances with grace. Typical in those days too, was the 'gents excuse' and the 'lady's choice.' When the MC announced a 'gents excuse', male partners on the floor could have their partners taken over with a tap on the shoulder by another dancer. The person so dispossessed would then sit down or seek another dancing partner. It was a strategy for allowing everybody to dance on occasions when the male dancers outnumbered the ladies. On other occasions, an MC would announce it just for the heck of it.

Another fun in the game was the 'lady's choice.' In this, the ladies on the hall were allowed to choose partners for a dance. It provided an opportunity for the ladies to assert an existing friendship or signal their intentions for one. During a round of 'gents excuse', Okulele had tapped the shoulders of a gentleman and swiftly danced away with his lady. During another round of 'gents excuse' Okulele tapped the shoulders of the same gentleman and made way with the same partner. When a round of 'lady's choice' was announced, the lady in question rewarded Okulele's attention with a request for a dance. This did not please the initial partner. The rapport between the lady and Okulele intensified during the course of the evening to the extent that the scorned gentleman, a CKC boy, left the hall. Other CKC boys were outraged, but the rules of the dance floor had to be observed. Decorum was maintained throughout the night.

In the days following this event, news came from the town that CKC boys, out of solidarity with their comrade, had planned to form gangs to waylay Bo School boys if the latter dared come to town. For two weeks, the Immaculate Four did not leave the campus because they did not want a confrontation. Then they forged a plan. They went to CKC when school was in session and asked to see the principal. Once in the principal's presence, they explained that they had thought of ways to reduce tension between CKC boys and Bo School boys. They claimed that their mission was to explore ways to minimize the tension generated by soccer and sports competitions and instead initiate ways for the two schools to cooperate. The principal was impressed by this and he gave them all his attention. They proposed joint scouting camps and cooperative debates comprising teams jointly made from the two schools. The principal was agreeable to this and promised them their support. They appreciated his time and promised to see him again with more details.

The meeting had lasted a good thirty minutes. It had attracted the attention of CKC boys who hovered around the

Office for news of this unusual visit. As the Bo School boys left, they let it drop that they had gone to alert the principal about the threat against them, in particular who was behind it. They had warned that they were prepared to defend themselves in whatever way and that the blame would be on that individual. They claimed that the principal had promised to monitor the situation. That defused the tension that had emanated from the activities of the Immaculate Four.

Attempt at Truancy

There were occasions when the classroom was not a welcome place. Usually, this followed a breach of a teacher's rule. In such cases, there was no place to hide on campus, if one wanted to escape a teacher. Our common ruse was to use the hospital. A common strategy to avoid going to class was to fake illness, go to hospital, and pretend that you were afflicted by the most horrible disease; something you hoped the doctor will not figure out and therefore order you to rest in your dormitory. You would then return to campus and pass the day the way you had planned it. It did not always work according to expectation.

I had fallen foul of our history teacher and, as usual, he had threatened to 'sit on me with double energy.' I decide to skip class that morning to avoid this 'double energy', whatever it meant. Another classmate, Sahr Fania, was in the same plight and had decided on the same course of action. That day we wrote our names in the 'sick report' book early in the morning. After the principal had signed the book, a group of us trekked to hospital. We reported first to the reception nurse whose duty it was to register us, record our temperatures, and then send us, one by one, to see the doctor. Most illnesses were from malaria and the temperature routine helped the doctor to diagnose it speedily. After several of my colleagues

Had been sent in to see the doctor, it was now my friend's turn at the nurse's station.

"What is your name?"

"Fania S."

"Your full name?"

"Sahr F."

The nurse wrote 'SahrFania.' She checked his temperature, wrote it on a piece of paper and ushered him to see the doctor on duty. Then it was my turn with the nurse. Hardly had the nurse finished recording my temperature when I saw SahrFaniah leave the doctor's surgery. He had a fazed look on his face, but before I could explore the reason, I was motioned into the doctor's surgery.

The doctor on duty that day was Dr. DrissaYilla, a no-nonsense old Bo School boy and a prominent member of the old boys' association. He knew the tricks of the truant, even from his own days in Bo School. I entered his surgery with tremendous confidence and presented mymedical form. He looked at me and looked down at the details on my paper. Then he asked me.

"And what's wrong with you?"

"I am suffering from neuralgia."

"Neuralgia, eh? And what is neuralgia?

"I recited the dictionary definition that I had strenuously but carefully memorized."

"What are your symptoms? What signs make you think you do not feel well?"

"Well, I had fever last weekend and my head ached the day before."

"Do you have fever now?"

"It is coming."

Dr. Yilla looked at the temperature the nurse had recorded: 98.4 degrees Fahrenheit.

"What you need are six lashes on your bare buttocks. There is

nothing wrong with you and you are wasting my time. If you do not hurry back to class, I'll come over and administer the lashes myself. By the time I leave you will be suffering from diarrhea. Neuralgia my foot!"
I quickly exited the doctor's surgery and ran back to class in the miserable company of SahrFania.

Competition and Cooperation

Excellence in academic performance was driven by competition and cooperation. In class one competed with other classmates for the top positions at the end of the year. In the dormitories, the blocks competed for the best academic block in each dormitory. The houses also competed for the 'house with best brains' or the 'best sportsmen on campus'. These competitions were characterized by a high degree of cooperation. Each member of a class or dormitory felt responsible for the other members. We studied hard and took each other to task for any perceived weakness. I learnt this the hard way.

Going into form four, my class faced the examination record of the previous form five. The preceding form five was working hard to be on top, and even though we were a good two years from taking the examination, we had determined that we would shatter the records of both classes. With the help of our teachers, we started monitoring and comparing our class averages with those of the two classes that had preceded us. We acquired every *legacy* (notes from previous outstanding students) that came our way and we studied them diligently. We were doing fine. At least I thought we were. I was doing my fair share of it until I flunked one crucial midterm test. My classmates attributed this to distractions in Bo Town as I had taken to bound-breaking quite a bit prior to this.

We proceeded on midterm vacation and returned to school with renewed enthusiasm. There was a laundry block by the dining hall. One Saturday, I went to do my laundry, which I did infrequently. I found three of my classmates there doing their own laundry. We started to joke and share vacation experiences. All of a sudden, the discussion took a sharp and bitter turn. Each student upbraided me for my poor performance in the previous midterm. It started as a joke, I thought. They became so acrimonious that I could not take it anymore. I had to leave the laundry block. In the days following, I felt ashamed of myself. I felt the guilt of letting the aspirations of the class down. I resolved to make up for it. I cut down on my bound breaking and took my studies seriously. When at the end of term I came first in the class, the same classmates rushed to congratulate me. "Good job, Lemmy."

"Thank you."

'If we had not put fire in your behind, you would be carrying the class bucket.'

"I knew you at St. Andrew's and knew you could do better than what you were doing."

"Right on target!"

"Thanks, guys."

I don't think even my parents would have done as well in motivating me to work that hard in School. Such was the solidarity among Bo School boys.

Paris Block 'C'

My story about my life in Bo School would be incomplete without paying deserving service to Paris Block 'C' and the merry men that lived there in my time. As miscreants such as Vassimu would say, "You cannot live in Bo School and not break the law. Not possible." The spices of life were the Saturday morning inspections, the *sunakatu* (breakfast for Muslims fasting that day), the inter-house competitions, both academic and athletic and, occasionally, the inter-house debates.

Who can forget the embroidery from the various girls' schools that adorned the beds of lucky boys, or the derision of the boys from the colony, Freetown, whose girlfriends could not provide such decorations to match? Who can forget the flowery language of sweet nothings that came in these items? 'Forget me not.' 'Love me little but long.' 'I love you as fishes love water.' How about the code names of these girls' schools: *Mesopotamia, The Equator, Capricorn?*

Njaluahun Girls Secondary School was *Mesopotamia*, because it was between two rivers, the Moa and Male Rivers in Sierra Leone (like the Euphrates and the Tigris). Harford Secondary School for Girls was *The Equator* because it was midway between Freetown and Bo, and Centennial Secondary School was simply *Capricorn* because it was south of Bo.

One weekend, choirs from the girls' schools had come to compete in Bo for the inter-secondary school singing competition. We knew that the girls from the three Christian schools would be made to go to church on the Sunday. We plotted to meet these girls in their respective churches. The main purpose was to send letters with them to other girlfriends who had not come to Bo.

There was a myth about Bo School. People believed that Bo School boys were not religious. Not true! The truth was that the school did not enforce any particular religion. It provided the opportunity for all to worship according to their faith, even those without faith. On Fridays, Muslims left the campus for Friday prayers in mosques of their choice. Similarly, on Sundays, Christians were allowed to leave

Campus and worship in their respective churches.

That Sunday, we deployed teams to the respective churches in various parts of town: the Methodist Church in Hangha Town, the United Methodist Church in New Site, and the United Brethren in Christ Church in Moriba Town. As I was devoted to a member of the Harford choir, I joined the team that went to the United Methodist Church in New Site, even though my regular church was the Methodist church in Hangha Town.

It was a sunny day. We all turned out in our Sunday best like suitors. We marched across town with the ostentation of a flock of peacocks. We arrived in church fairly early and took seats where we could easily see the Harford girls arrive and leave, even if they took the back seats. There were five of us and we fit neatly in one pew. The church was quite full that day as the Harford girls had added to the usual congregation and many families had come in solidarity to the Harford team.

The service was long that day, and with a crowded church, the heat was palpable. Throughout the service, whether we were sitting, standing, or praying, our eyes were across the aisle waiting to catch the glance of the one we loved. The girls in turn, under the watchful eyes of their chaperon, stole precious furtive glances our way, to our delight. In the midst of this, one of our members succumbed to the heat and dozed off in his pew.

The sermon that day was about maturity. The lesson was 1 Corinthians 13:11

When I was a child, I spake as a child, I understood as a child, I thought as a child: but when I became a man, I put away childish things. King James Version (KJV)

The pastor went into action, suddenly coming alive from his pre-sermon prayer. He got so spirited with his theme that I actually caught myself listening to him. In between my regular distractions, I followed him to the end. Then he ended with 'Let us pray.' At this point the church fell silent as we went into meditation. Then we heard an odious sound from our bench. A member of our group, who had slept all through the sermon, had farted! All eyes turned to our bench. All together we pointed at our sleeping companion who was blissfully unaware of his disgrace. Nevertheless we all felt the collective shame, and at the end of the service, disappeared from view as quickly as we could, forgetting the letters we had been so eager to give the girls earlier. From this episode, our friend earned the nickname 'Kondor Breeze', which he endured till we graduated from Bo School.

RAMADAN WATCH-NIGHT

Ramadan is the ninth month of the Islamic calendar. Muslims believe that it was in this month that the first verses of the Quran were revealed to Prophet Mohammad. Ramadan month lasts 29 or 30 days, or until the new moon is sited. It is the month in which practicing Muslims do not eat or drink during daylight hours. In Bo School, everybody was a Muslim during Ramadan and a Christian during Easter or Christmas. The attractions were the perks that came with each celebration.

During Ramadan, an early morning meal was provided for fasting Muslims who were allowed to eat before sunrise. In the evening, special dishes were added to their meal to help them transition from an empty stomach to a full meal. Many non-fasting students took advantage of these provisions and identified as Muslim for the duration of the Ramadan month. By far the most spectacular collaboration came in the form of the Ramadan festival. The night before 'Pray Day' which marked the end of Ramadan, groups held lantern parades through the city, the climax of which was the lantern competition that was held at the city center.

As in most things in Bo Town, Bo School led the rest. Each year, the town awaited the Bo School lantern and people were never disappointed. During the month, students would be dispatched to various settlements around the town to obtain bamboo and raffia palm. Others cut out different coloured paper. A team would meet and agree on the theme for the parade and a lantern figure to match it. The team would then be divided into procurers, builders, and musicians. The builders decided on the structure and estimated the materials they would need. The procurers group organized students to obtain these materials from the surrounding villages and farmsteads. One or two patrons would be called upon to finance essential purchases. The builders proceeded with the construction of the lantern as the material became available. The musical group was to compose or rework old tunes to match the year's theme. They would lead the performance on the 'watch night' once everything had come together.

Ramadan watch-night, also known as *Wutuba*, was a carnival. Small groups emerged from various communities in Bo Town jubilating around their lantern. The lanterns were always drawn from religious stories: like Noah's ark, or Abraham and the sacrifice of his son, or Adam and Hawa (Eve) in the Garden of Eden. Each paid tribute to the creative mind of its architects.

On *Wutuba* night, the night before the Eid prayers, the whole school gathered in front of the dining hall after dinner. While we waited for the night to get darker, we worked ourselves up into frenzy. When our spirits were high enough, our leaders let us out of the gates into town. The lyrics, *Who let the dogs out?* always reminds me of this night. Our regular route was through the western gate by the railway line, right by the staff quarters onto Tikonko Road. The leaders carefully regulated our pace.

We would go down Tikonko Road into town, with a stop at the clock tower. From here we took a roundabout route into town: up Prince Williams Street to the roundabout, left on Mahei Boima Road to Kissi Town Road, and left on Kissi Town Road to the town center. After the clock tower, we would make a courtesy call on Dr. Yilla, an old Bo School boy and a patron. Once there, our singers would choose specially composed songs to please our host. We would sing songs that praised his record in Bo School and his standing in Bo society. He was never disappointed. When he felt sufficiently flattered, *Kortor* would retreat indoors and emerge with a wad of currency notes, which he gave to our leaders. The group would change to a song of appreciation accompanied by intense stomping of feet and raucous sounds from all sorts of objects.

From *Kortor* Yilla's place, we stopped at the homes of other prominent Muslims whom we would praise and flatter in order to obtain generous donations from them. Most of the Muslims of worth were Madingo families who were prominent in town for their commercial or religious activities. They included the Turays of New Site and Hangha Town, the Kebbays of Kissi Town, and the Sesays of Kortugbuma. Some of our patrons were very generous, others less so.

Each patron got treated according to his or her generosity. If a donation was generous, our lead singers raised a composition to show appreciation. Usually, we implored Allah to be generous to that patron. If a donation was unsatisfactory, we left with a mocking song and dance such as, '*Nor put yukalangbapahn mi* (Don't put your body lice on me)'

Wutuba night was a rough night. Boys and girls prepared for it accordingly. Boys looked for old boots, especially military or police boots. They put extra studs

Underneath so they could create sparks when they struck them against asphalt roads. Girls doubled their clothing for protection against aggressive boys. They wore double jeans trousers and carried concealed pepper water for errant boys. Everybody danced their way toward the city center for the main event that usually happened far into the night.

The climax of the night was the award of the prize for the best lantern of the year. In my time, it always went to Bo School. After that, we danced our way back to campus with last stops at the Sesays of Kortugbuma, the Turays of Hangha Town, and the home of Jawara, a diamond tycoon from the Gambia. It would be in the early hours of the morning by the time we returned to campus. Back on campus, there would be a final vigorous jig before we went to bed. It would have been a night well spent. Whatever happened to all the monies collected was known only to the *Kpakos*, the senior boys in the group.

Chapter 8

CHANGING TIMES

In the '50s, Bo School was supreme in academics, athletics, quiz, and singing. In each annual competition, it could field two separate teams, one to compete with schools in the colony, the other to compete with schools in the protectorate. It would win first place in all the activities in each sporting arena. That was Bo School at its height. It was in my time, the early '60s, that things began to change. Other schools in Bo emerged to challenge its hegemony. One was Christ the King College (CKC), the other, the St. Andrew's Secondary School (UCC). Inch by inch both schools reduced Bo School's supremacy in football, athletics, and academics.

Yengema, the diamond mining town in the Kono District, was common ground for secondary school pupils around the country. Pupils from all over the country came to the mining town to visit relatives and to get assistance with their school expenses. This brought together boys and girls from Freetown and Bo, the main towns, and from the most renowned schools like Bo School, the Prince of Wales, and the Albert Academy. It was a great attraction for me because Uncle Kava worked there and there was good company during the holidays.

We came to Yengema eager to ride on the benefits that the reputation of our schools bestowed. In 1960 we, Bo School boys, arrived to find our position seriously undermined by one CKC boy, Nyademoh.

In the inter-secondary school soccer competition that year, CKC had trounced Bo School in a humiliating defeat. In Bo Town, we, Bo School boys, easily explained this as a fluke. We would teach them the following year, an explanation that seemed to have held sway in Bo Town. Elsewhere, it proved to be less so. Nyademoh had preceded us in Yengema by as much as four days. He had carried with him and distributed copies of the 'Daily Mail' newspaper depicting his school's defeat of the famous Bo School. The caption was undeniable, 'Nyademoh Scores Six Goals to Give CKC Victory over the Bo School,' it read.

For a while this sent us running for cover and out of competition for the attention of the girls. At a holidaymakers' dance, Nyademoh made the fatal mistake of trying to rub in his advantage to a group of girls in the presence of a junior Bo School boy. "Bo School is no more!" He showed off to his audience. "I alone, scored seven times against the whole team. They could not even return one." He teased.

"That is not surprising," the Bo School boy retorted. "After all, it just shows that your brain is in your feet."

The girls and all present laughed at this exchange. That effectively turned the table against the CKC boys and allowed us to regain our confidence. We held our heads up high once more and maintained it until the School Certificate results appeared the following year. CKC produced seven division one passes to Bo School's five. We continued in denial assuring all who could listen that 'We will deal with them next year.'

Bo School never accepted defeat.

The rivalry continued into the following year beginning with inter-secondary sports. I remember one athletics event that pitted our man against an upstart from my old school, St. Andrew's. Lennox Boyd our man was six feet two inches tall. His height had earned him the nickname, Lennox Boyd after Sir Lennox Boyd a similarly tall British foreign minister who had visited the school the previous year. Now, our Lennox Boyd was a braggart who epitomized intimidation. He represented the school in the javelin events.

His main tactic was psychological: verbal intimidation. It worked for him on most occasions. On this occasion it did not. His opponent was a William Wol.

William Wol came to St. Andrews as a refugee from the war in Sudan. He was sponsored by the World Council of Churches. In the athletics meet of 1961 he represented St. Andrew's school in the inter-school sports as the javelin thrower. When they met for finals, Lennox Boyd began his intimidating tactics.

"Heh. Fellow. So you throw the javelin?" He started.

"Yes." The unsuspecting Wol replied.

"Well here, you don't have a chance to win." Lenox Boyd went on.

"We'll see." Wol returned calmly.

"You can't win." Lenox Boyd insisted.

Wol said nothing. He just looked on as Lennox Boyd proudly displayed his javelin skills. After a while, Lennox Boyd paused and turned to William Wol.

"You see bloke, when I hold a javelin I look at it and I lean back to incline it at a particular angle. I gauge the angle until I reach angle theta. When I throw it from that angle, I throw it into infinity." He spoke as one measuring what he was saying, savouring every moment of his antics.

William Wol laughed, not impressed by this display. He responded.

"Meester. I don't know about angles and *difinity*, but I know about the spear and javelin. When I hold the javelin in my hands I see a spear and I look at my target as an antelope that I must kill, or an enemy carrying a gun. I must hit him before he kills me. So I throw my javelin as I would my spear to hit that target. You don't want to be that target. "

When the event was called, the field exploded with the St. Andrew's students chanting 'Wol! Wol! Wol!'' and the Bo School students, who believed they heard 'war', responding ''War! War! War!'' It was funny; neither group heard what the other was chanting. In the final event, William Wol defeated Lennox Boyd by several meters. Back among us, his schoolmates, Lennox said to us, "Gentlemen, that boy is phenomenal." With that he conceded victory knowing he would have to endure the teasing that would follow from us from then on.

By this time, the country was marching gingerly toward independence from Great Britain. A constitutional conference on the matter was convened in England from April 20 to May 4 1960. The outcome of this had been mixed. On the one hand independence had been successfully negotiated for the following year, 1961. On the other, a key member of the delegation had dissented from the terms of the agreement and had returned home with a determination to form a new party. This drama played out in school among the students. Each side had a significant following among students, often generating heated arguments in class whenever a teacher was absent. It was at this time that I met the chief minister who became the country's first prime minister after independence. He visited Bo School on his return from the independence conference and addressed a special assembly of Bo School boys. In his address, he admonished us against tribalism and commended the school for its nationalistic outlook. He left us with the words, "This country is yours. You should guard against tribal division. We are and must remain one country, one people." I was so moved that day that I made a commitment to that principle in matters relating to Sierra Leone. It has guided me through much of my adult life.

Independence came to Sierra Leone in April 1961 and

was celebrated with pomp. All school children in the town joined in a grand parade. We marched past the Chief Commissioner of the protectorate who took the salute. During lunch, we were treated to special meals and given souvenirs of the event. In the evening, we were allowed out for the ceremonies of the lowering of the Union Jack and the raising of the tricolour green-white-and-blue flag of the new Sierra Leone. These were preceded by colourful traditional dancing. The Prime Minister, my hero, was there and he thrilled the crowd when he joined in the *Wonde* dance just before the flag ceremonies. It was awesome! A memory forever etched in our minds.

Chapter 9

TRUST AND BETRAYAL

Roughing it with the Gang

During my last academic year at Bo School, certain events gave me insights into human behaviour and shaped my views on trust, friendship, and betrayal. One put me in hot waters with my Uncle Jusu, the other produced disillusionment about the school I had come to love so much.

In the second quarter of 1960, Uncle Jusu needed to refurbish his house. He sent money to me in Bo for windowpanes. I lived in Paris with a cousin and classmates, some of whom were close friends. The money was hand delivered two weeks to the end of term, too close, I thought, to do the required thing; that is, put it in the pupils' bank with the principal. I gave it to my cousin who locked it up in his box and had another friend lock my cousin's key in his own box. We were all convinced that the money was secure.

A week to the closing of school, I requested for the money from my cousin. We obtained the key from his friend and opened his box. To our shock, the money was gone. We raised the alarm and the block prefects searched everyone in the dormitory, with the exception of one person who was absent at the time. Distraught, I left the campus to explain my problem to my other cousin who lived in Bo Town. On my way, I saw Barrie, the student who was absent from the dormitory, purchasing goods, he said, for his grandmother. He was known to everyone to be destitute, and had been soliciting financial assistance to go home only days before. I continued on my way without raising any suspicions.

When I returned to the campus, Prefect Dimoh, a

senior prefect, invited me for a further interview. In the process, he asked if I suspected anyone. I named Barrie, a classmate, a dormitory mate, and a friend; I explained my reasons. I mentioned that I had seen him shopping in town as well as buying snacks during the football game that evening. I cited the fact that only a few days earlier, he had been begging for money. I acknowledged that Barrie was my friend but pointed out that only recently, Barrie was worried that he did not have money to go home for holidays. I concluded by saying that I could not explain how he had suddenly come into money. Prefect Dimoh dismissed me, cautioning me not to mention our conversation to anyone.

Early the following morning, several prefects entered Block C and asked the head boy to wake everybody up and have them stand by their beds. Within minutes it was done. Prefect Dimoh summoned the rest of the prefect body to meticulously search every student's corner. They went bed after bed until they reached Barrie's corner. Search of his box revealed some feminine items that seemed to have been recently bought and the sum of fifteen shillings. When asked to explain the source of the items, he claimed that they had been given to him to take home by a friend in Bo Town. He named the friend as Obediah, someone I knew very well. Prefect Dimoh decided to send for Obediah and asked Barrie and me to report to him after lunch.

During breakfast, the Lemmy Caution gang brainstormed the problem. We decided that there was circumstantial evidence that Barrie had stolen the money. We also suspected that he would try to contact Obediah before the latter reached the prefect. We devised a surveillance plan to forestall this. After breakfast, one person would man the eastern gate and another, the southern gate. I would keep a close watch on Barrie.

I pretended to continue eating while the scouts left for

their posts. It was not long before Barrie rose from his table and left the hall. I followed him. I saw Barrie head for London. I pretended to be going toward Manchester, an adjacent block to the east of London. I paused on a spot where I could see if Barrie exited through London toward Liverpool. My hunch at this point was that he was going to use an unconventional exit into town. I was correct!

Speedily, I went through Manchester and appeared on the other side of Liverpool just as Barrie was exiting from Liverpool and heading toward the swimming pool. Barrie hurried past the swimming pool without looking back. I pursued him fast. As he approached the swimming pool, he turned and saw me behind him. He dashed past the swimming pool toward the fence and leapt over it as I reached the fence. He was gone!

I felt defeated as I retreated to the compound to report to Prefect Dimoh what had happened. I could not believe my luck when, as I approached Paris, I saw Obediah cycling through the southern gate toward Paris. When he asked where he could find Barrie, I explained that he had left for the town but that the senior prefect wanted to see him.

In his interview with Prefect Dimoh, Obediah was very forthright. He denied giving any money to Barrie to the tune that he had claimed.

"I am very disappointed. Barrie has a history of stealing going back to his previous school where I first knew him. We had hoped that a school like Bo would have reformed him."

He wrote a short note to Barrie and left it with Prefect Dimoh. On his way out, he apologized profusely to me for what had happened, and wished me good luck in recovering the money I had lost. He added that I should prepare myself for the possibility that I might not.

On Barrie's return to campus, he was again summoned by

Prefect Dimoh. He stood by his earlier claim that Obediah had given him the money. Then Prefect Dimoh gave him Obediah's note. That immediately transformed him. He broke down in tears and asked Prefect Dimoh for forgiveness. He was now facing expulsion!

A place in Bo School was a privilege. Losing it did not only condemn a student to poor secondary education elsewhere, but also cast his family into shame and disrepute. For the remainder of the afternoon, and throughout that evening, prominent people arrived from Bo Town to plead with the Prefect Dimoh not to report the matter to the principal. In the end, Prefect Dimoh called me and asked my opinion.

My gang, and the rest of my classmates, had already deliberated on the matter and appealed to me to be lenient with Barrie. I had assured them I would. I now told Prefect Dimoh that I had nothing personal against Barrie, that he was indeed my friend, but that without the money, I would be in deep trouble with my uncle who was waiting for his windowpanes in the village. Barrie did not have the money, and so a settlement plan was agreed. He would bring the money after the holidays. As the saying goes, 'You can't squeeze water out of a stone.' Nothing could make Barrie produce the money before the holidays. I had no choice but to accept the agreement. As a result, I did not buy the windowpanes to take home

The saying that one good turn deserves another is seldom observed by some people. Barrie was one such person. When school re-opened, Barrie returned without the money he now owed me. He asked for an extension of time, and I was gracious enough to give it. A week to the agreed time, strange things began to happen to me. I was summoned from class one Monday morning by an angry Pa Smith and summarily expelled. Just like that! No explanation given. I was ordered to go to the dormitory and surrender my books and cutlery.

I returned to class to retrieve my books and I told my classmates what had happened. Nobody believed what had just befallen me. I was too stunned for any emotional response. Mr. Johnson our second math teacher, who had taught me at St. Andrew's, took the matter up with the principal. He learnt that that morning, Mr. Sanders had reported to the principal that he had opened his classroom and found insulting notes with my name and admission number on them. To Mr. Johnson, this scenario did not add up. It would be suicidal for any school boy to write an insulting note to a teacher and sign his name and admission number on it. It just did not add up. He asked to be allowed to look into the matter. By afternoon, he had convincingly demonstrated that the writing on the notes did not match mine; that someone was setting me up. With that assurance, I was again summoned to the office and reinstated. This was on a Monday.

On Wednesday, I was again summoned to the principal's office to face a very angry Pa Smith. "1XX3 Senessie, you are up to no good. You are not fit to be in this school. Now go and bring all your books and cutlery and leave the school. Today! I am sick and tired of complaints against you. Now leave my office. Go!"

Once again, I was too stunned to respond. I had not so much as been asked to defend myself. Whatever I was accused of was assumed to be true. Once again, I went to class to retrieve my books and I informed my classmates of the developments. This time the prefects got concerned when they heard the news. Prefect Dimoh was the first to volunteer to find out what the matter was. He learnt from the principal that a letter had arrived that morning from someone in Bo Town complaining that I had plotted with his children to harm Mr. Sanders. He wanted me restrained so as not to get his children into trouble.

Prefect Dimoh persuaded Pa Smith to allow him to investigate the matter further. He convinced him that since there was an address on the letter, it would be easy to trace the author and delve into his grievance. That morning, Prefect Dimoh dispatched separate people, one office messenger and one campus policeman, to visit the address in the letter and get the facts of the author's grievance. Each emissary returned with the report that there was no such address, and that there was no one by that name on the street in question. Faced with that evidence, Pa Smith summoned me again and reinstated me. I had set a record in the history of the school: I had been expelled twice in one week, and reinstated.

Mr. Johnson and the prefects were not willing to let the matter rest. After the 4 o'clock roll call, they called me to a meeting. Mr. Johnson asked me what my thoughts were on the matter. Was there was someone in the school or in the town who might be plotting against me? I told them that my only suspicion was Barrie who was due to pay what he owed me in five days time.

"Prefect Dimoh, can you take care of this? I know this boy from my days at St. Andrew's. He might be mischievous, but he is not malicious. We need to get to the bottom of this. See what you can do. Let me know if you need help."

Mr. Johnson handed Prefect Dimoh the letter and the notes that had so angered Pa Smith. Prefect Dimoh sent a policeman to fetch Barrie, with special instructions to bring all of his exercise books. He wanted to start by comparing handwritings. Before long, Barrie was brought to Prefect Dimoh along with his exercise books. As Prefect Dimoh began to inspect the exercise books, he noticed that Barrie was trying to retrieve one book. Thereupon, Prefect Dimoh snatched the book from him and proceeded to inspect it. He soon discovered that pages had been hastily torn from it. He lined up the two pieces of paper found in Mr. Sanders' classroom. They fit perfectly. He then examined the writing and found considerable similarities even though it was evident that attempts had been made at disguising the orthography. Another page proved to be the source of the note from the irate man in Bo Town. Prefect Dimohreported his findings to Mr. Johnson. In the morning, they went together to Pa Smith with their evidence. Pa Smith sent for Barrie's father and asked him to remove his son from the compound. I did not bother to ask after my money.

Conton

The school calendar was changed in 1960. Instead of beginning in January as it always did, it now began in September and ran till the end of June. This was to allow expatriates in the country to take their leave in summer when it would be warm in Europe. Thus the school year of 1960-61 had five terms, a period that proved too long for pupils and administration alike. The old man, W.D. Smith, also retired about this time. A new principal would be appointed to succeed him. The old boys argued that an alumnus be sought for the position; that anyone else would not understand the culture of the school which could be problematic. The Ministry of Education maintained that excellence and experience would be the sole criteria for any appointee. Events would prove that the old boys were right.

The 'wind of change' blowing through Africa was blowing through its institutions as well, especially institutions like Bo School. Pupils were exercising critical thinking, challenging authority, and developing a spirit of independence. To the old guard it was an age of rebellion in which long established authorities were being challenged. The spirit of independence that had seized the nation was running through its younger population, characterized by the challenge on corruption and emergence of oppositional viewpoints. In the midst of this a new principal was appointed to head Bo School.

He was a man noted for his erudition, eloquence and wealth of experience in education. In addition to his administrative responsibilities, he took on a teaching role. He taught the fifth form classes literature. His leadership style was different: less autocratic, appealing more to reason than to authority. He also had great interest in classical music. He would use the last ten minutes of his teaching each day to get the pulse of his pupils by having a discussion session. Students were encouraged to raise any issues they wanted in an atmosphere of frank exchange. The admiration his fifth form pupils had for him soon pervaded the rest of the school population. He became popular. Among the changes Conton brought to Bo was cultural diversification. Before him, most cultural activities were of the African experience, except those driven by the external examinations administered by Cambridge University. He revived the school choir with renditions of Negro spirituals and opera songs. He produced Shakespearean plays. For the Independence celebrations, the choir performed *Hiawatha's wedding* while the drama group produced Shakespeare's *Twelfth Night*. His students trusted him completely.

He was a principled man and wanted to instill these qualities in his students. He espoused values such as equality, honesty, and nationalism. However, he lacked understanding of protectorate realities and the circumstances surrounding the establishment of Bo School. By requiring parity in school fees between protectorate and colony students, he disenfranchised many protectorate students whose parents could not afford the incremental fees his policy imposed. This angered some old boys as well as those who fell victim to the changes he implemented. He had noted that the fees at Bo School were disproportionately lower than fees paid at other government institutions in the colony. To him this was unfair and he moved to address it. The old boys argued that raising the fees would affect the enrolment numbers at the school in the sense that most parents in rural Sierra Leone would not afford it. This was an argument he did not understand or agree with. Conton pursued his campaign of equal treatment between colony and protectorate pupils and got the Ministry of Education to authorize the increase if fees for Bo School. He announced the increase at the last assembly of the academic year. Slips would be sent out confirming the increase. Students were to return the slips to confirm that they would be returning to the school on the new terms. Those who did not return the slips would lose their places in the school. He did not factor in the unreliability of the postal service in the provinces. Many students did not receive the slips. They returned to the school, at the beginning of the new academic year, only to learn that they had lost their places. This, injustice, angered many in the Old Bo Boys Association (OBBA), who began to question whether the Conton was the right person for the school after all. They saw it as an assault of a colony person on the rights and privileges of people in the protectorate. A battle was beginning that Conton had no inkling of. It did not help him, as events bore out, that he did not understand the culture of the institution that he had come to head.

Conton had pride in his pupils and he demonstrated it whenever occasion demanded. He would have made the best principal Bo School ever produced. But as is often the case, many good leaders are destroyed by the surrogates they entrust with power and responsibility; in error they place them above the people they serve and are betrayed by them in the end.

Conton had appointed one of his senior teachers to supervise the kitchen. The job entailed procuring foodstuff for the kitchen and monitoring the quality of the food. Soon after this appointment, the quality and quantity of the students' rations deteriorated. In his classes, innuendos of these were emerging, but the students were not bold enough to make a direct accusation, and he did not have the requisite background to piece things together. Students in the sixth form were bolder. They invited the teacher in question to an open discussion in the dining hall. At this meeting, they stated their observations and their dissatisfaction. He explained that rats had eaten the rice and that this was responsible for the bad rice that had been cooked the previous day. He promised that it would not be repeated. Through the grapevine, it became known that this teacher had an outfit in town; he had a paramour who had opened a provision shop about the time that he had taken up responsibility for the school kitchen. Rightly or wrongly, students concluded that that was where their supplies were going. Anonymous articles were circulated ridiculing his explanation for the rice. In one article a cartoon depicted 2,050 rats eating rice. The number was the registration number of his car.

Students tried many times to convey events in the dining hall to Principal Conton but were unsuccessful in their attempts. One lunch time, the food was so bad that the students could no longer contain themselves. They marched directly to the principal with a bowl of soup as a specimen. Conton could not believe that that specimen had been served to the students. To him it was impossible. He saw it as an attempt by the students to discredit the master. He was annoyed at the student who carried this specimen and, in anger, acted out of character. He whipped the boy in his hand to teach him to be truthful. In the act, he caused a tear in the boy's hand. The group returned to the school and showed the cut in the boy's hand. Like a wild fire, anger spread through the student population.

In his literature class the following day, Conton brought the conduct of the boy up for discussion.

"Let me end today's discussion with a disappointment I had yesterday. You know, I have always admonished you boys to be honest, no matter what the circumstance, and to speak out on matters affecting you. Yesterday, I had a group of form one students in my office with a bowl of dirty water they claim had been served to them. They attempted to put the blame on the dining hall master. I expect you to pass on the virtue of honesty to your junior ones."

Although many in the class were annoyed at him, they did not show it. A few, like me believed that he was being deceived by his dining hall master; that he was as much his victim as they were. I attempted to shake this blind faith.

"Please sir. In this case, it was the boys who were honest. They were trying to tell you what is happening in the dining hall but you were not able to see it, sir." I said with some trepidation.

"You mean what was in that bowl was what they had been served to eat?"

"Yes, sir!" The class chorused.

Taken aback, Conton asked again.

"But how is that possible?" He asked, more to himself than to the class.

Then he itemized the budget provision for the school down to individual meals. He asked for detailsof our breakfast menu and was greeted with derisive laughter.

"You see, sir, yesterday was beans day. They served black eyed beans for lunch." I said.

"Yes, I could see some beans floating in the bowl." He replied.

"Well, what happens is that the sixth formers are served first. They get in their ration most of the palm oil that is cooked.

Then the *kondor* managers are served; then the fifth formers, and the fourth formers and so forth. By the time they get to the first formers there is little oil left. They simply add more water and salt. That is what you saw yesterday. Only that yesterday was worse than other days. In fact everything has been getting worse by the day." I explained. The class clapped in agreement.

When the class sensed that he was receptive to our views, we opened up some more, and a long discussion ensued, extending into the following period whose teacher was asked to cancel his class. At the end of it, Conton believed that there was something going on that he did not understand. He decided to look into the matter and promised us that he would address the whole school at midday the coming Saturday. Till then, he urged us to be patient and law abiding.

As promised, Conton addressed the student body on Saturday at 1 o'clock. There were two sections of the hall and the students sat according to seniority, form three and below at one end of the hall, form four to form fix at the other end. He turned from one to the other section as he spoke. Whenever he turned, a paper missile landed behind him. When his attention was drawn to it, he opened it and read it. Missile after missile contained grievances pertaining to the dining hall, especially the quantity and quality of the food. Details were given of how breakfast items had been substituted for cheaper and less nourishing alternatives. All allegations were signed by Black Arrow. He was torn between the trust he had in the dining hall master and what appeared to him to be the wild allegations of the students. His better judgment in the face of overwhelming allegations and the agitation of the students was to defer the matter and seek an investigation.

"Okay. Black Arrow has communicated your grievances to me. Give me some time to look into it.

Beginning next week, I'll be dining with you. That will give me an opportunity to know what is going on. Meanwhile, I will consult with the chairman of the board and advise that we set up a body to investigate your grievances."

That restored our confidence in him. We all agreed that he was not privy to the goings on in the kitchen and that when he experienced our grievances, he would do something about it. With that we accompanied him out of the hall with cheers and jubilation.

Conton had two children in the school. As matters stood, they were in solidarity with us, their comrades. Saturday was an outing day, when every student was allowed to leave campus from 1 o'clock till 4 o'clock when the roll was called.

Like most students, the Conton children visited their parents. They narrated the food situation on campus to sympathetic ears. The story goes that as they were returning to campus, their mother gave the younger one a dish to take along. He took the soup to dinner and shared it with some of his tablemates. This annoyed others on the table and the rumbling began.

It quickly spread through the dining hall that the Contons did not want their children to eat bad food and had given them food to substitute for the bad *Kondor*. Unexpectedly, it was the smallest boy in the school who started the stampede that followed. He flipped his plate of rice on the table saying "This is not fair!" Another on the same table joined in, "No! This is not right." Spontaneously, others on the table followed suit and joined in chorus "No! Not right" This spread quickly through the dining hall.

When it got to the senior section someone yelled, "Conton must go!" Others now took up this chorus and everyone was shouting, "Conton must go!" In this frenzy we poured out of the dining hall, through the southern gate into the town, all the while singing, "Conton must go!"

The school was at the heart of government policy. Never in its history had such developments been recorded. News got to parliamentarians. Powerful voices, especially among the alumni of the school, the old Bo boys, got involved and demanded a full investigation. It was argued that, not being an old boy, Principal Conton never understood the temperament of the school.

The man driving the old boys was the man who had engendered the students' grievances in the first place. In this crisis, he had seen an opportunity to align the old boys behind him, in case Conton was removed. In the end, some students were expelled for inciting behaviour, others were suspended. Conton was relieved of his position and transferred to headquarters as chief education officer. I believe that, to his grave, Conton never understood how all of this had happened; how the noblest of his intentions had turned out the way it did. I lost most of my friends after this event. Some were expelled; others were withdrawn by their parents to other schools.

Following Conton's departure, an acting principal was appointed and school was reopened. The acting principal was one of the worst teachers on the staff, the brightest academically but the laziest in teaching. It was as if the system rewarded poor performers. With this new change, a small band of us from the graduating class returned to finish form five. We were broken in spirit but were determined to plod on. Morale was low among us, to say the least. The ambition we had nurtured to beat the previous year's graduating classes had all but fizzled, as some of our best students had been dispersed to other schools. They would confer their credit to rival schools in the nation. At the end of the year, we slogged through our examinations to lackluster results. Thus the dream of our class outshining preceding classes fizzled into oblivion.

Epilogue

In 1976, a significant number of my classmates returned to Bo School for the annual OBBA celebration. We came as doctors, lawyers, engineers, and university lecturers. We cracked old jokes, recalled old memories, and traded our post-Bo-School experiences. We concluded that life in Bo School was good after all. We congratulated ourselves that considering our experiences, we had turned out just fine.

OBBA that year was overshadowed by two events: the execution of Dr. Fornah and eleven others since the last OBBA, and a political cloud that was looming on the horizon. 949 Fornah, was an exemplary old boy whose academic excellence had remained unmatched since he graduated from the school. His record used to be on display at every annual OBBA meeting, especially on prize-giving days. He had been an inspiration to most. He was executed for political reasons on July 19, 1975, hardly four months after the OBBA of that year. In our cohort groups we discussed the letter that had cost him his life. He had written to the country's first megalomaniac dictator thus:

Dear Prime Minister (Siaka Stevens),
In 1967 Sir Albert brought this country to the brink of political and economic disaster. All right thinking people realised that Sir Albert's insatiable desire for power and wealth spelt chaos and complete disruption of our social fabric. What he wanted to impose upon this nation was a one man dictatorship, shrouded by a fraudulent Republican Constitution that concentrated all powers in the hands of a single person. In view of this menace to personal freedom and economic stability, I accepted the call to service, and, left what you knew to be a very lucrative medical practice to join the fight against that political monster.
As leader of the Opposition then, you spearheaded the fight against this

menace. All of us who followed you accepted your profession of a deep attachment to the tenets of democracy and the rule of law. As you also know, when the Military unwarrantedly usurped the machinery of Government and imposed a Military dictatorship on the people of this country, you found me more than willing to risk life and limb to restore Parliamentary democracy to this beloved country.

It is nearly three years now since we assumed the reins of Government. Over this period I have had the opportunity of working closely with you. Many mistakes have been made during this period but till lately I had assumed that these were mistakes of the head and not of the heart. I now know that I was wrong. You have revealed an uncanny dexterity at manipulating weak and untutored minds both at Cabinet and Party levels. Your conduct of state affairs is in line with your Trade Union experience, a mixture of trite jokes cajolery and even violence. The introduction of the continuation of cold and calculated violence into the politics of this country poses a major threat to the social and political unity of this country. You are fully aware of the events I refer to. The shootings at the Freedom Press with the resultant death of an innocent child have never been investigated to the satisfaction of the thinking public. The wanton destruction of life and property at Ginger Hall during the Freetown City Council elections was as unprovoked as it was unnecessary. As usual the innocent, the very innocent children, were the sufferers. Again, the nation has waited in vain for an explanation. More recent, but no less serious, are the dastardly events in Port Loko. The heinous crimes committed there I put squarely at your door-step. I know, as you do, that you were the evil spirit behind them. I have spared no pains both in and out of Parliament to condemn the use of force and violence as a means to power. This is one fundamental area of disagreement between us.

A Constitutional Review Commission has been set up. It is now at work. In the interval, with you presiding, a so-called National Executive of the APC passed a resolution in favor of an Executive Presidency with all the powers of the state in the hands of one man. You yourself have never hidden your ambition to be such a President. You set the ball rolling at the meeting I refer to. I vividly recall the continuous tussle between you and Protocol Officers about the playing of the National Anthem for you. His Excellency the Governor-General has on more than one occasion been subjugated to serious embarrassment as to the use of the National Anthem when both of you attend the same functions. This display of infantile vanity may appear trivial, but to me with a trained medical mind, they are the manifestations of a megalomaniac syndrome. It is the top of the iceberg submerged below a sea of personal shyness. This coupled with an insatiable thirst for power can only spell disaster to this country. I now realize that no method will be too mean for you to achieve this goal. On my return from the USA and Britain I made my views on this matter very clear to you. I made it clear, that should you insist on this course of action and bring a bill to Parliament based on an Executive Presidency I will have no choice but to oppose it with all the forces at my command. As usual with you, the answer to a major issue was not enlightened discussion but the over-used joke.

I have noticed that our differences over financial policy have deepened with time. The Cabinet reshuffle of May this year was precipitated by the refusal of then Minister of Works and myself to sanction the dumping of six million Leones of the taxpayers money in the construction of a rock filled road less than two miles long. This project, as I indicated in a letter to you, had neither economic merit nor did it stand to ease the traffic congestion which was the pretext for its conception. Suppliers credit and pre-finance have a limited scope in the public finance of an under-developed country. Its misuse and abuse led to the near national bankruptcy of 1966-1968. You yourself have condemned the practice in your radio broadcast to the nation. I have always maintained that pre-financing should be limited to a small area of projects which will contribute to the social well-being of our people. Among this category are the provision of clean pipe borne water and the expansion of our radio services. In my discussions with World Bank and IMF officials I have indicated our general agreement with them not to engage in unnecessary pre-financing. You yourself have re-assured the World Bank along similar lines. Recently I have noticed that rejected pre-finance schemes are being dusted and brought to Cabinet without my Ministry being given an adequate opportunity to make its comments on them. During my brief absence on a tour of duty you signed a contract against the advice of my officials for pre-financing the purchase of armored vehicles costing nearly Le700,000. At a time when soldiers are badly housed I wonder whether your priorities as Minister of Defense are in the right order. The Military were never given an opportunity to say yes or no to this scheme. Recently you brought forward an elaborate scheme for police and army communications equipment. If accepted, it will cost this nation Le2.8 million. What I find curious is that the communication officers of both army and police put their requirements at Le300,000, roughly a tenth of the cost of your Pye advisers. The curious combination of an unrelenting drive to an Executive Presidency, armored vehicles to be manned by a specially selected troops primarily loyal to you, indicate that you intend to impose your will on the people of this country. You have never failed to equate yourself to SekouToure, Kaunda or Nyerere. Sierra Leone is a different country Mr. Prime Minister and to be frank you are not a Kaunda or a Nyerere.

In other areas, policies are equally confused. We all know the repeated use of troops and police for the eviction of the stranger elements from Kono, but as the country knows, this has become a cyclical exercise. You drive them with fanfare but quietly allow them to return for reasons that you alone can understand. There is no coherence in Government policy, no definitive co-ordination of Government policies, no firmness in the execution of Government policies. Your Kono exercise cost this nation Le600,000 extra for the army and police in 1969. The bill for the latest exercise is still to come. In the meantime most of the Lebanese expelled by this exercise have now been allowed by you to return. If our scanty resources cannot be used to create gainful employment for our people, then, as I have always pointed out to you Sir, we are now witnessing [a] form of highway robbery. These are problems that will not be solved by armored vehicles or over-expensive communication equipment.

I have written at length so that the nation will understand. I am painfully aware that my resistance to these schemes has not gratified me to you. Yet I owe it to myself and to my country to do my duty as I see it.

I had intended to attend the very important meetings of Commonwealth Finance Ministers at Nicosia and of World Bank and IMF at Copenhagen, but I am reliably informed of your intention to withdraw my accreditation to these conferences on your return. The honor of this country is a matter of supreme importance to me and I would not allow you to ridicule this nation now as you have done in the recent past.

Finally, let me warn the nations of the World that should their citizens allow you to embark on a pre-finance spree in the terminal days of your regime this nation reserves the right to disallow these debts in the future.

With all these strains and fundamental differences on principles and policies I realise that my usefulness in this Government under you has reached a low ebb. I cannot sacrifice principles for position, but as I always say, let history be my judge. I therefore wish to tender my humble resignation as from today.

Yours sincerely,

(sgd.) Dr. M. S. Forna.

Did he needlessly throw his life away? Would anything come out of his example? In a culture of subterfuge and betrayal, what could be expected? We agreed that he had done the right thing; that he had lived and died like a true Bo School boy. His was a true demonstration of the motto of Bo School: Manners Maketh Man.

That evening, a short tribute was paid to him by another luminary: Samuel Bangura of the central bank who was to die years later under mysterious circumstances: a suspected victim of a brutal and unscrupulous regime. On OBBA night, all old Bo School boys were equal and the seniors (the *Ngohs* or *Kortors*) went to tremendous lengths to make it so. The climax of the evening was the dash for the goat meat. There you saw company managers, bank directors and similar dignitaries, people who could afford ten times the goat that was served that evening, scrambling for a piece of it along with folks much younger than them. Such was the appeal and grandeur of OBBA.

The second shadow over OBBA of '76 was the growing disaffection in the country with the economic and political direction. There was restlessness across the country brought on by dissatisfaction with the government. In the end, we all agreed that there was little one could do and that the best course of action was to let events take their course. And so they did. In January, 1977 university students initiated a demonstration that spread nationwide when school children across the nation joined in. For a moment everyone thought the government would fall as the demonstrations brought the nation to a halt. But the president of the country, ever the masterful politician was able to bring the situation under control using various means. The events of that year propelled the country into a one-party state. The students who had foreseen it and sought to defeat it were betrayed by their adult counterparts.

As usual, OBBA 1976 included a cricket match between the old boys and the new. Traditionally, this was a match with a preordained result: a draw. On this occasion, an upstart in the new boys' team decided to upstage the old boys. He decided to play to win. 'What was it that he did not understand about this tradition?' When the old boys' team recognized this young man's game, they strategized to frustrate his effort. In the end the game was a draw, but the young man had drained the energies of the players on the old boys' team. As was tradition, OBBA ended with a dance on its last night. That again, created lots of opportunities for reunion, not only with old schoolmates, but contemporaries in Bo Town who had become the current dignitaries or VIPs in town. Indeed, our generation had come into its own.

Late in the afternoon of the following day, I paid a last visit to the campus. I did not know when next I would be there as I had an overseas journey ahead of me. I ran into three contemporaries who had succumbed to the same desire. Together, we toured the campus recalling memories that each spot triggered: the dining hall, the laundry, the dormitories, the French Field, Lamu, the assembly hall complex, the classrooms, the gates, yes the gates! The thrill of bound-breaking! The trials and tribulations on this compound as well as the joys and accomplishments; the bonds forged that had endured so far and promised to continue! We looked at the young students who were preparing to leave for their Easter holidays with no inkling of what the future held for them; just as we had been, in our time, after OBBA ceremonies, only that they came much younger these days. In our hearts, we felt the sentiments of the school song:

> *Bo School beloved*
> *Our alma mater dear...*

Other books by the author

Gomna's Children

A Corner of Time

Climbing Lilies

SIERRA LEONEAN WRITERS SERIES

Focusing on academic, fictional, and scientific writing that will complement **other relevant materials used in schools, colleges, universities and other tertiary institutions**, the Sierra Leonean Writers Series (SLWS) aims to promote good quality **books by Sierra Leoneans, writers of Sierra Leonean descent from around the world, and writers writing on or about Sierra Leone**. Even if the initial readership is made up of people outside Sierra Leone, it is the publisher's hope that students and other readers in Sierra Leone will eventually be at least some of the primary beneficiaries of these new works. Not only will people in Sierra Leone be able to read materials that relate to their own lives and experiences, budding writers will also be able to draw inspiration from the efforts of their compatriots and other established writers.

Submitted work undergoes a rigorous peer review process before being accepted for publication, with an international editorial board providing guidance to writers.

For further information, please visit our website:
www.sl-writers-series.org

Prof. Osman Sankoh (Mallam O.)
Publisher, SLWS
publisher@sl-writers-series.org

Ms Fatmata Sankoh
Business Manager, SLWS
Fatmata.Sankoh@sl-writers-series.org
Writersseries.sl@gmail.com

Published Books

A. History and Political Science

SLWS H&PS-1
Joe A. D. Alie, 2007
ISBN: 3-9808084-5-9
Sierra Leone Since Independence –
History of a Postcolonial State

A stimulating and informative account of Sierra Leone's political history from the last years of British colonial rule to the present. The book discusses some of the forces that have tended to unite and disintegrate the nation, paying particular attention to the deeds and misdeeds of the political elite. It concludes with an analysis of the major challenges facing Sierra Leone in the post-conflict period, as well as the prospects for building a progressive, democratic, peaceful and viable nation-state.

B. CREATIVE WRITING SERIES
SLWS CW-1
Osman A. Sankoh, 2001
ISBN: 3-00-003978-3

Hybrid Eyes – An African in Europe
This semi-autobiography critically examines the experiences of Africans and other minority communities in Germany as well as key values and stereotypes that many people in Africa hold about Europe. The author acknowledges the flaws of African culture and advances proposals for the way ahead.
SLWS CW-2

Sheikh Umarr Kamarah, 2002
ISBN: 3-9808084-0-8

Singing in Exile and The Child of War

This collection of poems examines the causes of the African (Sierra Leonean) condition, evaluates the African immigrant's situation in the West, hints at the role and culpability of Corporate West in African wars and woes, and concludes that African must ultimately assume the responsibility of rebuilding their continent.

SLWS CW-3
Abdul B. Kamara, 2003

Unknown Destination
ISBN: 3-9808084-1-6
The book examines a wide spectrum of challenges that confronted African students in the aftermath of the economic reforms or structural adjustments of the 1980s, and the concomitant hardship that swept across Africa. The author uses his own real life-experiences to compare student life in the East as experienced in China, with that in the West (Germany), and adroitly analyses what these unforeseen cultural divergences implied for young Africans in search of higher education.

SLWS CW-4
Samuel Hinton, 2003

The Road to Kenema
ISBN: 3-9808084-3-2
In *The Road To Kenema* Samuel Hinton presents a poignant, sometimes searing portrait of a man who stands with one foot

planted firmly in the ageless soil of Africa, the other on the promise-filled shores of America. Balancing memories of his homeland with dreams of his adopted country, Hinton takes his reader on a journey that is often upsetting, but always engaging. Each poem beckons, almost forces, the reader to experience the situation at hand...

SLWS CW-5
Karamoh Kabba, 2005

Morquee – The Political Drama of Wish over Wisdom
ISBN: **3-9808084-4-0**
Morquee traces Sierra Leone's turbulent recent history through the eyes of one of the individuals caught up in it. With its patient description of how an innocent young man can become tangled in a web of corruption, deceit and war, *Morquee* is a microcosm of the post-colonial experience in much of West Africa. *Morquee* is part of a renaissance in Sierra Leonean story-telling. The Sierra Leonean Writers Series is at the forefront of this movement. With this publication, Karamoh Kabba cements his status as a bright young hope for the Sierra Leonean novel. Home-grown creativity in Sierra Leone is on the rise again.

SLWS CW-6
Yema Lucilda Hunter, 2007

Redemption Song
ISBN: **3-980-8084-6-7**
Told partly through the diaries of Emmanuel Martin, a boy on the threshold of adulthood, *Redemption Song* is the story of how war came to a peaceful, if impoverished, country and tore it apart. However, as Emmanuel grows up and his life unfolds, all is not doom and gloom...

SLWS CW-7
Mohamed Combo Kamanda, 2007

The Visa
ISBN: **3-980-8084-7-5**
The Visa is a lucid, informative, educative and humorous
play; it is truly a "travel ticket" into the two cultures: the
Western Culture which shocks and transforms many
Africans upon their arrival in Europe, and the African
culture with its own uniqueness – you may call it a clash of
cultures, races and value systems. The play touches on these
issues in a light-hearted manner. ...

SLWS CW-8
J Sorie Conteh, 2007

In Search of Sons
ISBN: **3-980-8084-8-3**
In this book, J. Sorie Conteh tells the universal story of the
preference many societies/cultures in Africa have for more
sons in the family than girls. The story is set in the author's
country, Sierra Leone, and tells the harrowing experience of a
mother who tries to fulfil her husband's desire for more sons.
She becomes pregnant but eventually dies in labour *in search of
sons...*

SLWS CW-9
Michael Fayia Kallon, 2010
The Ghosts of Ngaingah
ISBN: 978-9988-1-3983-4
This is a story full of superstition, yet so credible. When a
people neglect that which constitutes their collective
consciousness and that which helps them to grow and
prosper as a community, the negative effects are bound to
hit them hard.

SLWS CW-10
J Sorie Conteh, 2011
Family Affairs
ISBN: 978-9988-1-3984-1

In *Family Affairs* J. Sorie Conteh returns to the fictitious town of Talia which featured in his previous book novel, *In Search of Sons*. Once again he has dealth with the stresses, strains and even tragedies that can arise within families when time-honoured beliefs and expectations are challenged.